SMITHSONIAN INSTITUTION
BUREAU OF AMERICAN ETHNOLOGY

THE MYTHOLOGY OF THE BELLA COOLA INDIANS

BY

FRANZ BOAS

WASHINGTON
GOVERNMENT PRINTING OFFICE
1898

II. — THE MYTHOLOGY OF THE BELLA COOLA INDIANS.

By FRANZ BOAS.

PLATES VII–XII.

CONTENTS.

PLATE VII.

EXPLANATION OF PLATE VII.

⁎ Cross-hachure indicates black; vertical hachure, red; horizontal, blue; diagonal, green; dots, orange; white, natural color of wood.

Fig. 1.—Mask representing Senx (front and profile). Natural color, nostrils red, eyebrows black. Height, 29 inches. Cat. No. $\frac{16}{1185}$.

Fig. 2.—Mask representing Aɪk'untā'm (front and profile). Natural color, nostrils red, eyebrows black. Height, 30 inches. Cat. No. $\frac{16}{1180}$.

Fig. 3.—Mask representing the Singer of the House of Myths. Blue, red, black. Height, 15 inches. Cat. No. $\frac{16}{1184}$.

Fig. 4.—Mask representing Snūɪk'ulx·ā'ls (front and profile). Natural color, black. Height, 23 inches. Cat. No. $\frac{16}{1123}$.

Fig. 5.—Mask representing K·x·ēx·ēk·nē'm (front and profile). Natural color, black. Height, 13 inches. Cat. No. $\frac{16}{1122}$.

Fig. 6.—Mask representing Six·sēk·ɪlai'x· (front and profile). Natural color, black. Height, 31 inches. Cat. No. $\frac{16}{1115}$.

Fig. 7.—Double mask representing Nusnē'neq'als (opened, closed, and profile of inner mask). Inner face, red, blue, and black; inner side of wings, black and red; outer face, black, red, blue. Height, 14 inches. Cat. No. $\frac{16}{1116}$.

Fig. 8.—Mask representing Snoō'ɪexeɪts Aɪk'untā'm (the deer). Nostrils and mouth, red; forehead and eye region, blue; eyebrows, eyes, nose, black; rest, natural color. Height, 9 inches. Cat. No. $\frac{16}{1126}$.

Fig. 9.—Mask representing Snitsma'na. Natural color, black, spots blue, lines red. Height, 9½ inches. Cat. No. $\frac{16}{1119}$.

Fig. 10.—Mask representing Aiaɪilā'axa (front and profile). Black, blue, red. Height, 10½ inches. Cat. No. $\frac{16}{1120}$.

Fig. 11.—Mask representing Aiaɪilā'axa (front and profile). Red, green, black. Height, 10 inches. Cat. No. $\frac{16}{1121}$.

Fig. 12.—Mask representing S'anōɪx·muɪa'lt. Natural color, black, orange. Height, 9 inches. Cat. No. $\frac{16}{1117}$.

Fig. 13.—Mask representing S'anōɪx·muɪa'lt. Blue, black, red, natural color. Height, 10 inches. Cat. No. $\frac{16}{1117}$.

Masks of the Bella Coola Indians.

PLATE VIII.

EXPLANATION OF PLATE VIII.

。*。 Cross-hachure indicates black ; vertical hachure, red ; horizontal, blue ; white, natural color of wood.

Fig. 1. — Mask representing Maɪapǎ᾿litsėk᾿ (profile and front). Black, red, blue. Height, 28 inches. Cat. No. $\frac{1}{1}\frac{6}{4}\frac{6}{2}$.

Fig. 2. — Mask representing Yula᾿timōt, and details of ornaments attached to head-ring. Black, red, blue. Height, 31 inches. Cat. No. $\frac{1}{1}\frac{6}{4}\frac{6}{1}$.

Fig. 3. — Mask representing Maɪ᾿apē᾿exoėk᾿. Black, red, blue. Height, 9 inches. Cat. No. $\frac{1}{1}\frac{6}{4}\frac{6}{3}$.

Fig. 4. — Mask representing Iɪ᾿iɪu᾿lak. Black, red, blue. Height, 10 inches. Cat. No. $\frac{1}{1}\frac{6}{4}\frac{6}{7}$.

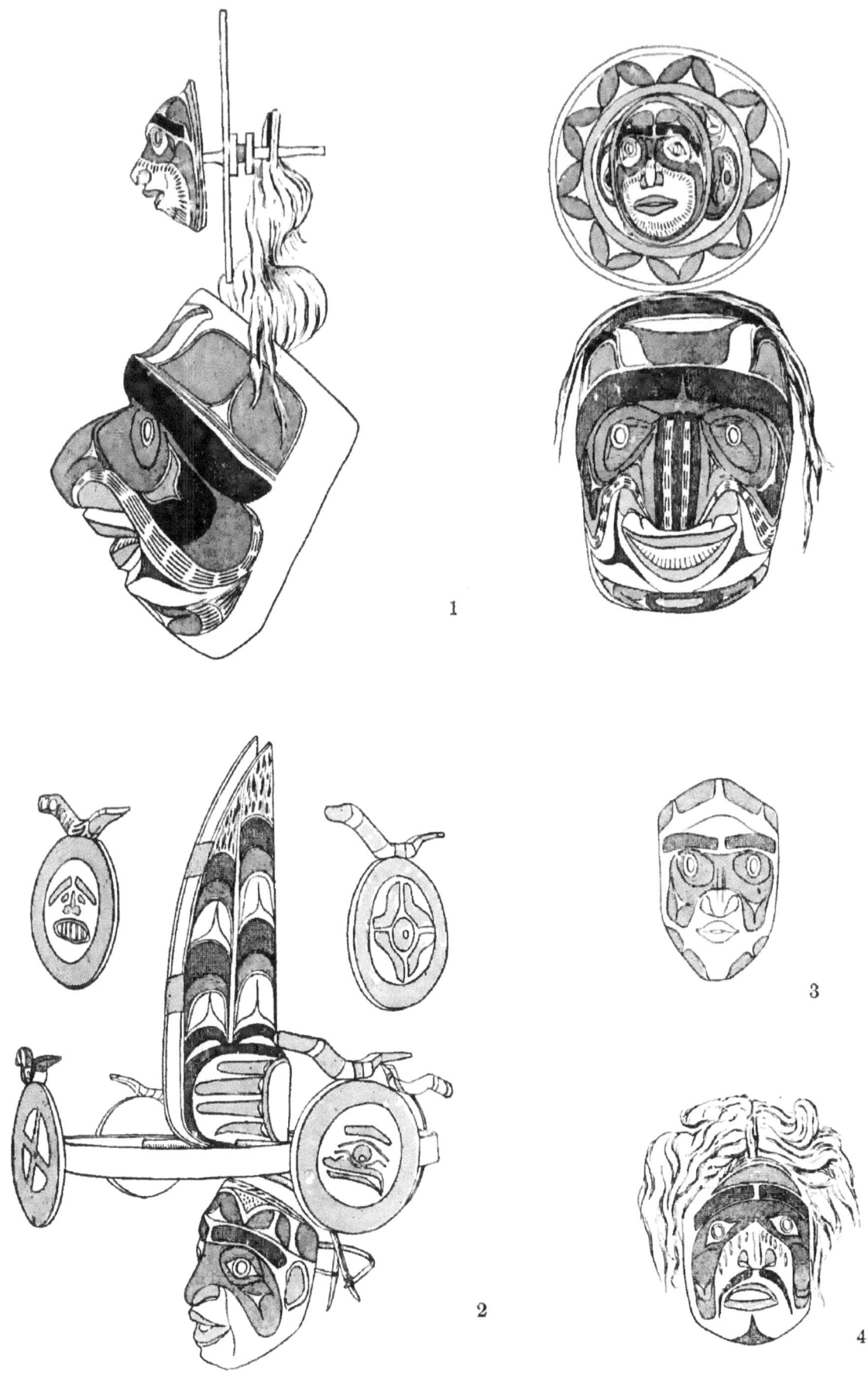

Masks of the Bella Coola Indians.

PLATE IX.

EXPLANATION OF PLATE IX.

Fig. 1.—Mask representing Xēmxēmalā'oɹla (front and profile). Design: full moon. Natural color, black, red. Height, 13½ inches. Cat. No. ₁₁₈₀₀.

Fig. 2.—Mask representing Xē'mtsiwa (front and profile). Design: full moon. Natural color, black, red. Height, 12 inches. Cat. No. ₁₁₈₀₁.

Fig. 3.—Mask representing Ōmq'ōmkī'lik'a (front and profile). Design: half-moon. Natural color, black, red. Height, 12 inches. Cat. No. ₁₁₈₀₀.

Fig. 4.—Mask representing Q'ō'mtsiwa (front and profile). Design: half-moon. Natural color, black, red. Height, 12 inches. Cat. No. ₁₁₈₀₂.

Fig. 5.—Mask representing Ai'umki'lik a (front and profile). Design: stars. Natural color, black, red. Height, 12 inches. Cat. No. ₁₁₈₀₀.

Fig. 6.—Mask representing Kᵘlē'lias, wearing a ring of red cedar-bark (front and profile). Design: rainbow. Natural color, black, red. Height, 14 inches. Cat. No. ₁₁₈₀₀.

Fig. 7.—Mask representing Q'ulaxā'wa (front and profile). Design: salmon-berry blossom. Natural color, black, red. Height, 12 inches. Cat. No. ₁₁₈₀₇.

Fig. 8.—Mask representing Ā't'mā̈kⁿ (the kingfisher). Wings at sides of head, tail over the forehead. Natural color, black. Height, 12 inches. Cat. No. ₁₁₈₀₀.

Fig. 9.—Mask representing ʟ'ētsā'apleɹāna, wearing a ring of red and white cedar-bark (front and profile). Design: grease-bladder. Natural color, black, red. Height, 14½ inches. Cat. No. ₁₁₈₀₀.

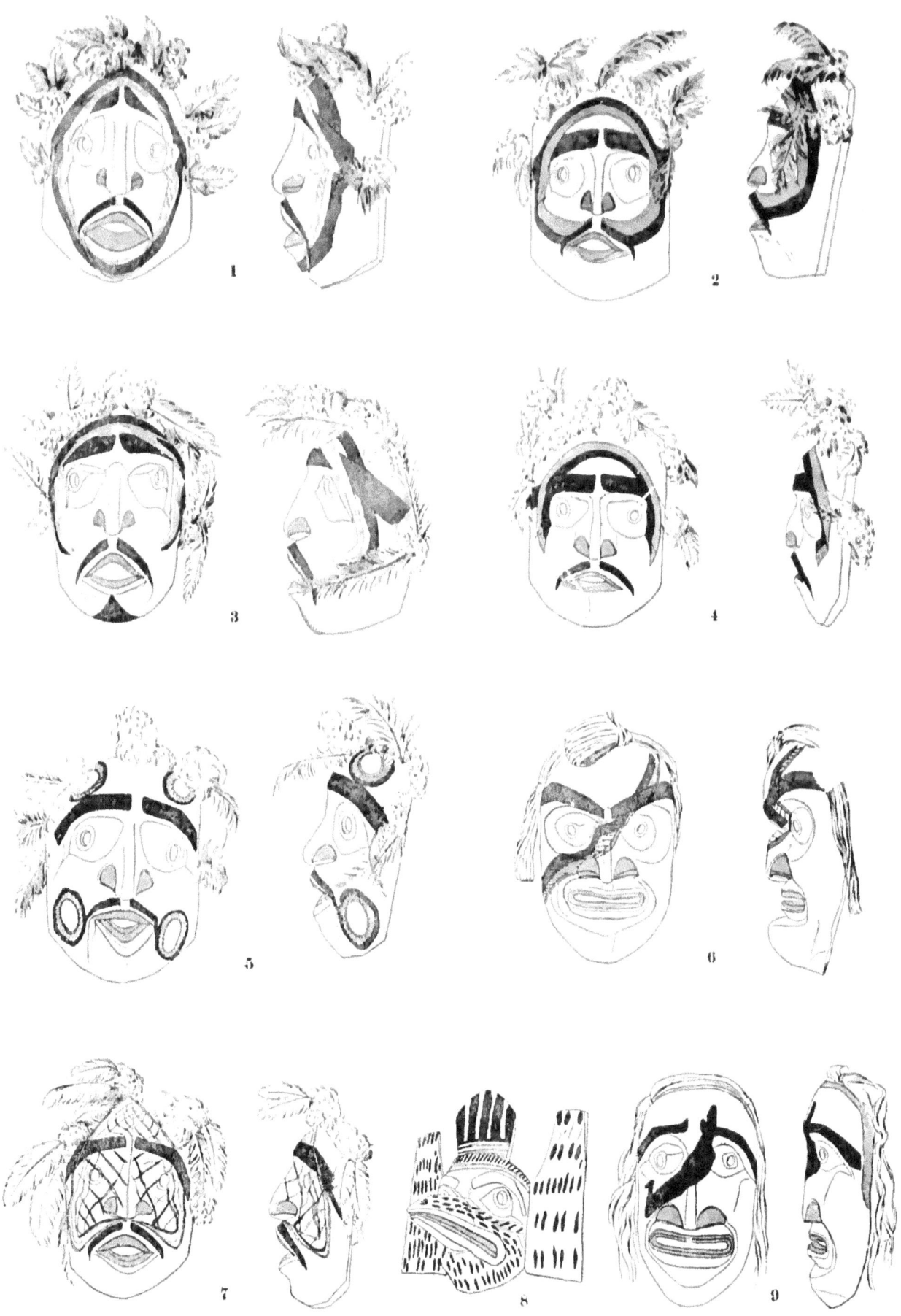

Masks of the Bella Coola Indians.

PLATE X.

EXPLANATION OF PLATE X.

*** Cross-hachure indicates black; vertical hachure, red; diagonal, green; white, natural color of wood, except in cases where the whole mask is black.

Fig. 1. — Mask representing Naqumiqa'otsaix. Black, red; ornamented with red cedar-bark. Height, 16 inches. Cat. No. $\frac{16}{441}$.

Fig. 2. — Mask representing the Bear of Heaven. Green, black, red. Height, 12 inches. Cat. No. $\frac{16}{433}$.

Fig. 3. — Mask representing Aʟk x'ē'ʟnɛm (front and profile). Natural color, red, black, green. Height, 8 inches. Cat. No. $\frac{16}{432}$.

Fig. 4 — Mask representing Aiq'oa'yosnɛm (front and profile). Natural color, black. Height, 9½ inches. Cat. No. $\frac{16}{441}$.

Fig. 5. — Mask representing Aiq'oa'yosnɛm (front and profile). Natural color, black. Height, 9½ inches. Cat. No. $\frac{16}{440}$.

Fig. 6. — Mask representing Aiq'oa'yosnɛm (front and profile). Natural color, black. Height, 9½ inches. Cat. No. $\frac{16}{442}$.

Fig. 7. — Mask representing Nonō'osqa, before the birth of the flowers (front and profile). Greenish with faint reddish spots, black. Height, 9 inches. Cat. No. $\frac{16}{447}$.

Fig. 8. — Mask representing the shaman of Nonō'osqa (front and profile). Black, white streaks under eyes. Height, 10 inches. Cat. No. $\frac{16}{1425}$.

Fig. 9. — Mask representing Nonō'osqa, after the birth of the flowers (front and profile). Natural color, black. Height, 9 inches. Cat. No. $\frac{16}{443}$.

Fig. 10. — Mask representing A'ʟʟ'âʟg·ila (the moon). Natural color, black. Height, 16 inches. Cat. No. $\frac{16}{441}$.

Fig. 11. — Mask representing attendant of Nonō'osqa (front and profile). Natural color, red, black. Height, 11½ inches. Cat. No. $\frac{16}{1426}$.

Fig. 12. — Mask representing the Black Bear. Natural color, green, red, black. Length, 15 inches. Cat. No. $\frac{16}{1601}$.

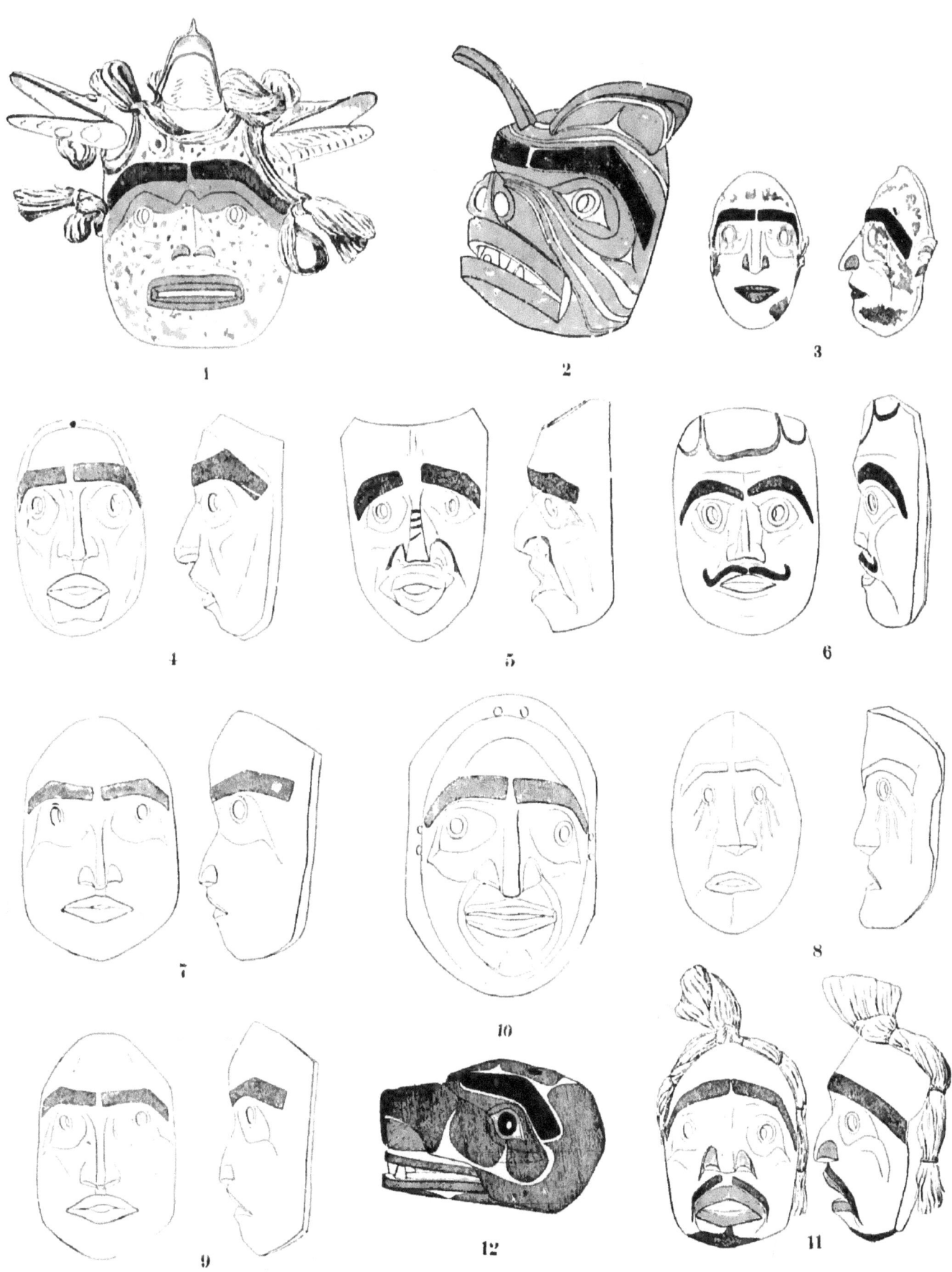

Masks of the Bella Coola Indians.

PLATE XI.

EXPLANATION OF PLATE XI.

.*. Cross-hachure indicates black ; vertical hachure, red ; horizontal, blue ; dots, orange ; white, natural color of wood, except in cases where the whole mask is black.

Fig. 1. — Mask representing the thunder-bird (front and profile).   Black, red.   Height, 11½ inches.   Cat. No. ₁₁⁶₄₃.

Fig. 2. — Mask representing Aʟxulā'tɛnum (front and profile).   Ornamented with red cedar-bark.   Orange, blue.   Height, 12 inches.   Cat. No. ₁₁⁶₇.

Fig. 3. — Mask representing the rabbit.   Set with mountain-goat skin.   Natural color, black.   Height, 13 inches.   Cat. No. ₁₁⁶₅₄.

Fig. 4. — Mask representing the owl.   Black, red.   Height, 12 inches.   Cat. No. ₁₁⁶₅₀.

Fig. 5. — Mask representing Lō'qots (the mountain).   Natural color, black.   Height, 19½ inches.   Cat. No. ₁₁⁶₄₆.

Fig. 6. — Mask representing the raindrop.   On top of the mask is a long switch set with feathers, only the lower part of which is shown.   Natural color, black.   Height, 10 inches.   Cat. No. ₁₁⁶₅₆.

Fig. 7. — Bird-shaped implement worn by a companion of the thunder-bird.   It is filled with eagle-down.   During the dance it is shaken, and the down flies out of the holes in the lower part of the implement and from the back.   Length, 18 inches.   Cat. No. ₁₁⁶₅₂.

Fig. 8. — Mask representing the sea-monster K·'ī'ʟxˑta.   Red, blue, black.   Height, 19 inches.   Cat. No. ₁₅⁶₅₂.

Fig. 9. — Mask representing the spirit ʟaʟaiā'iɪ.   Black, orange, set with bear-skin.   Height, 9 inches.   Cat. No. ₁₅⁶₅₅.

Fig. 10. — Mask representing the hermaphrodite (front and profile).   Natural color, red, black.   Height, 11 inches.   Cat. No. ₁₅⁶₅₂.

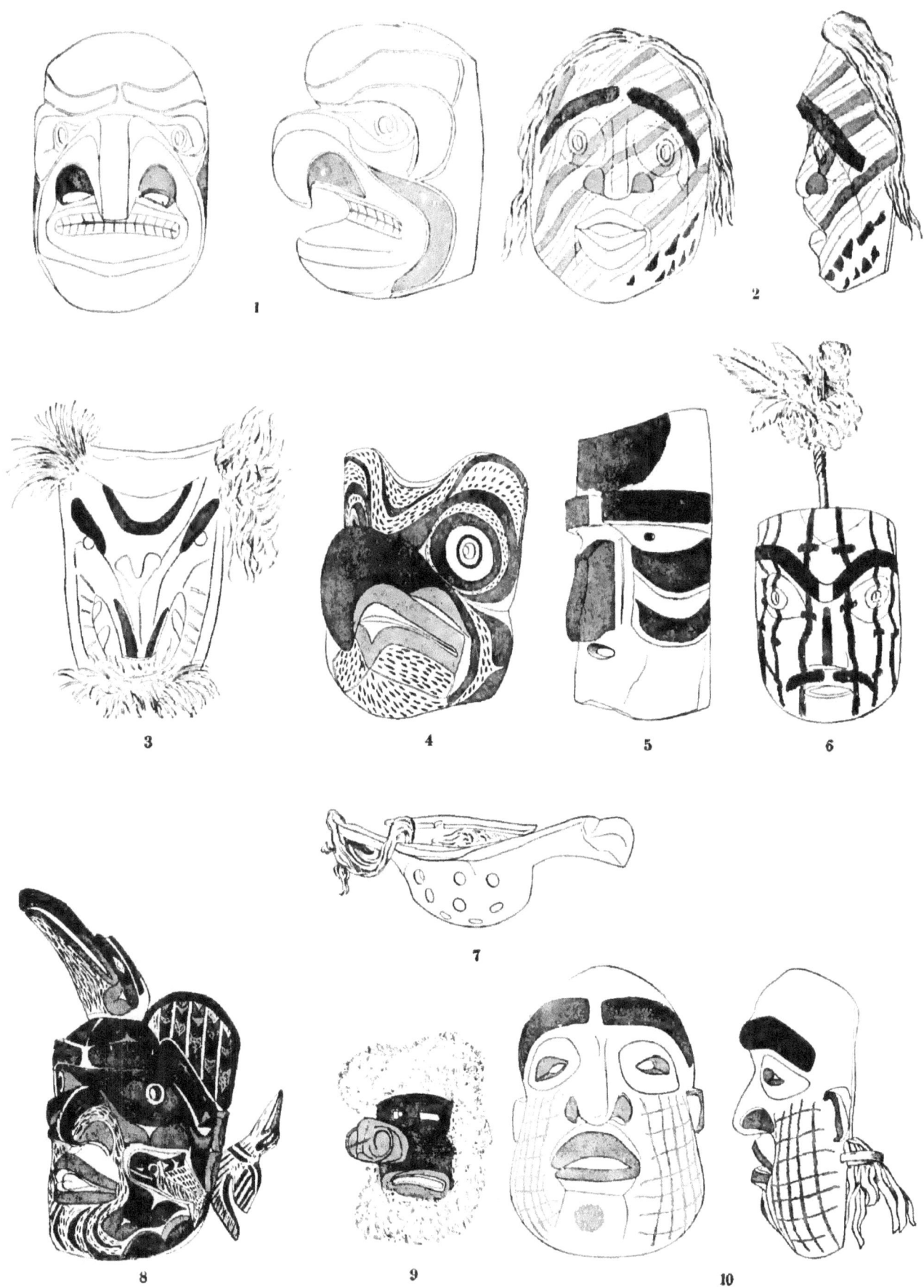

Masks and Carving of the Bella Coola Indians.

PLATE XII.

EXPLANATION OF PLATE XII.

Fig. 1. — Mask representing Anaūlikuts'ai x̄ (front and profile). Natural color, black. Height, 10 inches. Cat. No. $\frac{16}{717}$.

Fig. 2. — Mask representing Anaūlikuts'ai'x̄ (front and profile). Natural color, black. Height, 11 inches. Cat. No. $\frac{16}{1457}$.

Fig. 3. — Mask worn by the Cannibal dancer (front and profile). Natural color, black, red. Height, 13 inches. Cat. No. $\frac{16}{1454}$.

Fig. 4. — Mask worn by the assistant of the Cannibal dancer. Blue, red, black. Height, 10 inches. Cat. No. $\frac{16}{1459}$.

Fig. 5. — Mask worn by the assistant of the Cannibal dancer (front and profile). Blue, red, black. Height, 10 inches. Cat. No. $\frac{16}{1456}$.

Fig. 6. — Carving representing the S'ā́ʟpsta in the shape of an eagle. Red. Length, 11 inches. Cat. No. $\frac{16}{1164}$.

Fig. 7. — Carving representing the S'ā́ʟpsta in the shape of a wolf. Red, black. Length, 12 inches. Cat. No. $\frac{16}{1163}$.

Fig. 8. — Mask worn by the assistant of the S'ā́ʟpsta (front and profile). Natural color, black. Height, 8 inches. Cat. No. $\frac{16}{1165}$.

Fig. 9. — Mask worn by the Ōlx (front and profile). Red, blue, black. Height, 14½ inches. Cat. No. $\frac{16}{1450}$.

Fig. 10. — Club carried by the Ōlx. Red, blue, black. Length of head, 7 inches. Cat. No. $\frac{16}{1150}$.

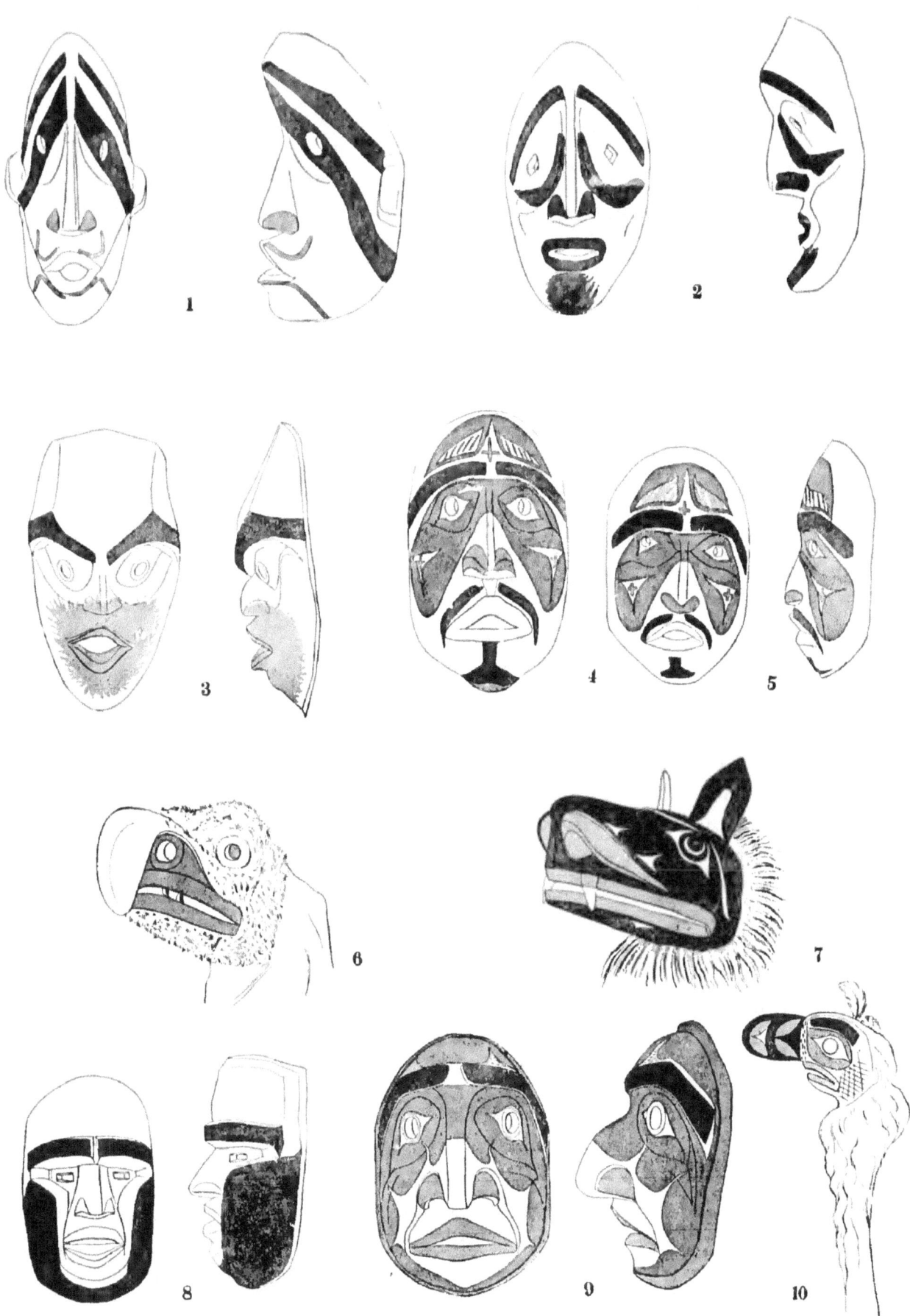

Masks and Carvings of the Bella Coola Indians.

I.

The Bella Coola are a small tribe inhabiting the coasts of Dean Inlet and Bentinck Arm, two long and narrow fiords situated in about latitude 52° north, in British Columbia. Their habitat extends along Bella Coola River, which empties into North Bentinck Arm. The name "Bella Coola" is a corruption of the word "Bílxula," by which name the tribe is known to the Kwakiutl. There is no term in their own language embracing all the tribes speaking the Bella Coola language. It seems that at a former time the tribe was quite populous; but, owing to various epidemics and the introduction of other diseases, its numbers have dwindled down, so that at the present time it has been reduced to only a few hundred souls. The language spoken by the tribe belongs to the Salishan family, more particularly to the group of dialects spoken along the coasts of Oregon, Washington, and British Columbia. The great similarity between the Bella Coola and the other Coast-Salishan dialects leads me to assume that at one time the tribes speaking these dialects inhabited contiguous areas. At the present time the Bella Coola are separated from other tribes speaking Salishan languages by a considerable stretch of country, which is inhabited by tribes of Athapascan and Kwakiutl lineage. Vocabulary and grammar have been highly modified, particularly by an extensive elision of vowels. The relation of their language to the other dialects of the Coast Salish is similar to that of the Tillamook, another language belonging to the Salishan family, which is spoken on the coast of Oregon, in an area separated from the rest of the Salishan territory by the district inhabited by the Chinook.

Physically the Bella Coola bear evidence of long-continued contact with the northern Coast tribes, and also with the Athapascan tribes of the interior. Evidently intermarriages have been quite frequent, so much so that their present physical appearance differs considerably from that of the southern Salishan tribes, of whom they form a branch. The same is true in regard to their customs and beliefs, which differ fundamentally from those of the southern Salishan tribes.

In the present paper I shall describe the mythology of the Bella Coola, and discuss its development.

II.

Our previous knowledge of the mythology of this tribe is based on studies made by Adrian Jacobsen, Fillip Jacobsen, Goeken, and the writer. In 1886 I published a few brief notes on their traditions.[1]   Goeken pub-

---

[1] Verhandlungen der Berliner Gesellschaft für Anthropologie, Ethnologie und Urgeschichte, 1886, p. 206.

lished some remarks on the religious life of the Bella Coola in 1886,[1] which, however, contain so many misconceptions that they cannot be used to advantage. At the same time I published a brief description of the tribe, based on information received from a small group of members of the tribe who were travelling in Germany. In this description also there are a number of misconceptions. The Indians were shown a collection of masks from Vancouver Island with which they were not familiar. They gave, however, explanations of these masks, judging by the similarity to masks of their own tribe ; consequently the explanations given there are not correct.[2] In 1890 I fell in with a number of Bella Coola who were fishing for salmon in Fraser River. The information obtained from them was published in the reports of the British Association for the Advancement of Science, 1891.[3] A. Jacobsen published a description of their ceremonies in 1891.[4] Fillip Jacobsen described some of their traditions and customs in 1894 and 1895.[5] I published a collection of traditions in 1894 and 1895.[6]

III.

All the collections which have been made heretofore do not bring out clearly the principal characteristic of the mythology of the Bella Coola. The tribes of the North Pacific coast consider the Sun as the most important deity, but at the same time they believe in a great many beings of supernatural power. For this reason their whole mythology is very unsystematic. The Bella Coola, on the other hand, have developed a peculiar mythology, in which a number of supernatural beings have been co-ordinated. A system has been evolved which justifies our terming the supernatural beings "deities." The general features of this system are as follows : —

The Bella Coola believe that there are five worlds, one above another. The middle one is our own world, the earth. Above it are spanned two heavens, while below it there are two underworlds. In the upper heaven resides the supreme deity, a woman who interferes comparatively little with the fates of mankind. In the centre of the lower heaven, that is in the zenith, stands the house of the gods, in which reside the Sun and all the other deities. Our own earth is an island swimming in the ocean. The underworld is inhabited by the ghosts, who are at liberty to return to heaven, whence they may be sent down again to our earth. The ghosts

[1] Original-Mittheilungen aus dem königlichen Museum für Völkerkunde, Berlin, 1886, pp. 183-186.
[2] Ibid., pp. 177-182.
[3] Seventh Report of the Committee on the Northwestern Tribes of Canada, pp. 2-18 ; Report of the 61st Meeting of the British Association for the Advancement of Science, held at Cardiff, 1891, pp. 405-449.
[4] Verhandlungen der Berliner Gesellschaft für Anthropologie, Ethnologie und Urgeschichte, 1891, pp. 383-395.
[5] Ymer, Tidskrift utgifven af Svenska Sällskapet för Antropologi och Geografi, 1894, pp. 187-202 ; 1895, pp. 1-23.
[6] Verhandlungen der Berliner Gesellschaft für Anthropologie, Ethnologie und Urgeschichte, 1894, pp. 281-306 ; 1895, pp. 189-195.

who die a second death sink to the lowest world, from which there is no return.

The upper heaven is called Atsa'axl, or Snutx·lok·a'ls ti Sōnx· t'aix·, or Sōnxaul Omq'ō'mkilik·a. The deity ruling there is a woman who is called Qamā'its, or Tsi sisnâaxīl ("our woman"), or Ek⁰!yak·imtōls'īl ("afraid of nothing".

This heaven is described as a prairie without any trees. It is said that in order to reach it one must go up the river from the house of the gods in the lower heaven. In another tradition it is said that in travelling from the lower heaven to the upper heaven one has to pass the rent in the sky which is called Tsʟna'lōtas ti Sōnx· t'aix·. The house of the supreme deity stands in the far east, and a gale is continually blowing over the open country, driving every thing towards the entrance of her house. Near the house, however, it is calm. In front of the house stands a post in the shape of a large winged monster, and its mouth is the entrance to the house. In front of the house-door there is gravel of three colors, — blue, black, and white. Behind the house is a salt-water pond in which the goddess bathes. In this pond lives the si'siuʟ or xtsaltsalō'sᴇm. This being sometimes descends to our world. Wherever it moves, the rocks burst, and slide down the sides of the mountains. It is described as a snake or a fish (see pp. 44, 66).

In the beginning of the world the mountains were of great height. They were human beings who made the world uninhabitable. Qamā'its made war upon the mountains. She vanquished them, and made them smaller than they used to be. During this fight she broke off the nose of the mountain Yūlyuʟᴇ'mʟ, which is situated near Nuʟ!ᴇ'l. Its face may be recognized even now; and the Indians say that when its name is called, it answers. There are two mountains near the head-waters of Bella Coola River. The one is called Sʟex·ʟêkoai'ʟ; the other one, Na'axʟ. The former had a fire, called Snutai'k·nimsta, burning in his house. This fire warned him of the approach of enemies. When Qamā'its made war upon the mountains, the fire warned its master. Qamā'its was coming down the river in her canoe, which is named "T!kun." When she approached, he broke her canoe, and she returned to heaven. The canoe has been transformed into stone, and may be seen to this day at the foot of the mountain Sʟex·ʟêkoai'ʟ. It is said that Qamā'its visits the earth every now and then. Her visits cause sickness and death. She is described as a great warrior.

In the centre of the lower heaven, which is called Sōnx·, stands the house of the gods. This house is named Nusmᴇ'ta (the House of Myths), or Nusk!oaʟtnai'x·sta ("where man was created"), or Nusk·ʟaʟnᴇ'msta ("the house from which people come down"), or Nusqulxoai'x·sta ("the house to which people go"). In front of the house stands a post called Nuʟtnē'k·ta. It is painted with representations of all kinds of birds. A white crane (?), Qô'xôx, is sitting on top of the post. The master of the house is Senx, the Sun. He is also called Tā'ata ("our father"), or Sınai'yakila ("the sacred one"), or Smayalō'oɪla. It seems that he is the only deity to whom the Bella Coola pray. They do not pray to Qamā'its, the deity of the supreme heaven. I have not found any prayers directed to the other deities of the lower heaven. I recorded a number of such prayers directed to the Sun. They are as follows : —

Aɪk·!x·iɪō'ɪsux Tāatau'! ("Look on us where we are going, Father!")

Tāatau'! aɪk·altx·omdō'ɪx! ("Take care of us, Father!")

Tāatau'! ɪk·altxumtō'ɪx ala mentaɪt'a'ts! Tāatau' aɪēp'alōsaɪtōɪx! ("Father! take care of our road! Take care of us!")

After a long-continued rain, they pray : —

Tspōsɛ'mx Tāatau'! kōɪ'ié'lxustimō'tx, Tāatau'! ("Wipe your face, Father! that it may be fair weather.")

The mountain-goat hunter prays : —

Ōsqa yūstūtānx, Tāatau', ta mɛnmɛ'ntsnō, Smāyalōɪlau'! ("Let your children look at me, Smayalōɪla, Father!")

A person pursued by misfortune prays : —

Nuqlamēk·ī'mtsx Tāatau'! anuqomak·ma'tō ti q!ayanɛmtnɛmt'ai'x·. ("Make me happy, Father! You have given me too much misfortune.")

A sick person prays : —

Nuqlamēk·ī'mtsx Tāatau'! sk·a sasq!oalostō'mx Tāatau'! ("Let my life be long, Father!")

The successful hunter, or the woman who has found a plentiful supply of berries, prays : —

Nōnōqalamē'k·tuts ti mānɪt'aix· sk·a nōqlamēk·imts sk·a pōɪtus anoai'k·mēts'ats sk·ētsk·is ti sq!aitst'aix·. ("Father! You make me happy. You give me what I desire. Thus I find what I wished for.")

The Bella Coola also make offerings to the Sun. Hunters throw four small slices of seal-meat, of mountain-goat tallow, etc., into the fire as an offering to the Sun, in order to obtain success in hunting. Sick people burn parts of their clothing, which they decorate with red cedar-bark, as an offering to regain health.

The second deity, who is called Aɪk'untā'm, seems to be of equal importance. Senx and Aɪk'untā'm stay in the rear of the House of Myths. Near the fire stays Snūɪk'ulx·ā'ls. He is an old man who formerly ruled over the House of Myths, but who has given up his place in favor of SENX and ALk'untā'm. These two might be called the rulers of mankind. In most traditions they are described as trying to destroy man, notwithstanding the fact that they are considered the creators of mankind. This peculiar characteristic of these deities is clearly brought out in the traditions recorded on pp. 78 ff. In one legend which I collected in 1890, ALk'untā'm's mother, Nūnusōmik·ceqonē'm, is described as a Cannibal, who inserts her long snout in the ears of man, and sucks out his brain. Eventually she was transformed into the mosquito.[1] I did not hear her mentioned as one of the deities residing in the House of Myths. According to the same tradition, the salmon were obtained by a man who gambled with ALk'untā'm, the stake being the salmon. ALk'untā'm lost, and the man took the salmon down from heaven. Another legend of the origin of the salmon is recorded on p. 38, where it is told how the birds obtained the salmon. According to still another tradition (p. 94), the Raven obtained the salmon by marrying a salmon girl. In the tradition quoted above, ALk'untā'm also gives to man the power to cure disease by means of the water of life, which the shaman sprinkles on the sick person.

A number of inferior deities live in the House of Myths. They might be called the assistants of the principal deities. In order to understand their functions, it is necessary to state that the deities residing in the House of Myths have particular charge of the religious winter ceremonial of the Bella Coola which is called kū'siut, and which corresponds to the ts'ētsā'eqa of the Kwakiutl. I have described this ceremonial, and its importance in the social life of the Kwakiutl, in another paper.[2] The kū'siut is of equal importance to an understanding of the social life and mythology of the Bella Coola. It is sufficient to say at this place that the ceremonials performed during the kū'siut are mostly dramatic representations of myths referring to the various deities, particularly to those of the House of Myths: therefore masks representing these deities are used in the ceremonials. Plates VII to XII[3] show a series of these masks. Figs. 1, 2, and 4 (Plate VII) are SENX, ALk'untā'm, and SnōLk'ulx·ā'ls. The functions of many of the inferior deities seem to refer solely to the kū'siut. These deities and their functions are as follows: Six·sēk·ilai'x· (Plate VII, Fig. 6) ordains the death of man and animals. According to one statement that I received, there are four deities of this name in the House of Myths. It is his particular duty to kill those who transgress the laws of the kū'siut. This deity is mentioned by Jacobsen, who calls him Sek-seik Kallai.[4] Nusnē'neq'als (Plate VII, Fig. 7), or the Snēnē'iq of the House of Myths, sits by himself in one

[1] Verhandlungen der Berliner Gesellschaft für Anthropologie, Ethnologie und Urgeschichte, 1894, p. 293.
[2] Report of the U. S. National Museum, 1895, pp. 311–738.
[3] Drawings by Mr. Rudolph Weber.
[4] Verhandlungen der Berliner Gesellschaft für Anthropologie, Ethnologie and Urgeschichte, 1891, p. 388.

corner of the house. He prevents those who are not initiated in the secrets of the kū'siut from approaching the house. The Snēnē'iq is a fabulous monster, the peculiarities of which are described in a number of traditions (see pp. 83 ff.). S'anŏLx·mṇLa'lt (Plate VII, Figs. 12 and 13) is a boy who performs kū'siut dances all the time. When the deities resolve to send a new dance down to our world, it is conveyed by S'anŏLx·mṇLa'lt. It is the office of another deity to sing, accompanying the kū'siut dances of the gods (Plate VII, Fig. 3). Anuqat'ŏ'tsEm is a deity in regard to whose functions I have not been able to obtain detailed information. It is said that he intervenes on behalf of man when SEnx and ALk'untā'm threaten to punish him. There are two goddesses in the house who also intervene in favor of man when the principal deities threaten him with death and sickness. Their names are Snitsma'na (Plate VII, Fig. 9) and AiaLilā'axa (Plate VII, Figs. 10 and 11). They wake man after sleep. Without their help, nobody could wake from sleep. AiaLilā'axa is at the same time the guardian of the moon. Every month she restores the moon to her full size, and she cleans her face after an eclipse. The moon is called A'nL'āLg·ila (Plate X, Fig. 10). The eclipse is produced by several deities called ᴀiq'ᴇa'yosᴻEm, which means "painting the face black" (Plate X, Figs. 4–6). It is believed that at this time the moon performs one of the most sacred ceremonies of the kū'siut, which are thought to be very dangerous to the performer. The black paint with which her face is covered is supposed to be a protection against these dangers. AiaLilā'axa cleans off the paint after the dance has been completed. According to Jacobsen,[1] the Indians say that during an eclipse the moon (En-kla-loi'-killa) paints her face black. The same deities are believed to paint and to clean the faces of human kū'siut dancers. Snitsma'na and AiaLilā'axa also resuscitate those who are killed by the dangerous performances of the kū'siut.

While the functions of the beings enumerated here are mostly concerned with the kū'siut, others are more immediately concerned with the affairs of the world. Important among these is K·x·êx·êk·nē'm (Plate VII, Fig. 5). SEnx is the creator of man, but his work is supplemented by that of the god K·x·êx·êk·nē'm. When SEnx creates a new-born child, K·x·êx·êk·nē'm gives the child its individual features. Before children are born, the goddess named Nuêx·qEmalsai'x· or SēᴇsēmE'ltstas SEnxalā'oLEla places them in a cradle and rocks them. After she ceases rocking them, the children are sent down to our world. She also rocks the young of all animals; and when she stops, SEnx sends them down to our world to be born. At the same time he ordains that their skins and their flesh shall serve for clothing and food for man. Nuêx·qEmalsai'x· might therefore be called the deity

[1] Verhandlungen der Berliner Gesellschaft für Anthropologie, Ethnologie und Urgeschichte, 1894, p. 112.

having charge of the birth of all animal beings. While she is rocking the cradle, she sings, —

"xoĕsχoĕsmaïχ'nïmȫta nĕkȫ k's ʟa nȫĕχ'ʟ!ɛ malsaïχ au au au au.
Aayotsĕtsk'ȯχ'ats siχ 'ïχȫʟayä'mk'tĕts'ats snɛmnɛmk·'ä ʟtowasȫats ayawa
sȫyȯnχsȫats au au au au."

Another deity living in the House of Myths is the mother of flowers, called Nonȫ'osqa (Plate X, Figs. 7 and 9), the daughter of Snukpa'nʟits. It seems that this last name means "going to the right." This evidently refers to the fact that the Sun is believed to move on his path towards the west, face forward, and consequently during the spring months ascends the sky moving towards the right; so that Snukpa'nʟits, moving to the right, means at the same time the springtime, when the sun is moving up the sky. This is the time when flowers begin to sprout. Every spring Nonȫ'osqa gives birth to all the plants in the order in which they begin to appear. A shaman is called to her aid by two old women who assist her (Plate X, Figs. 8 and 11).

Every year, at the time of the winter solstice, the deities determine who shall die during the ensuing year. Two beings called Kakĕstsai'ȫʟ ȫʟa xmä'noas are placed on the ends of a long plank, which is supported at its centre, and swings like a seesaw. Then all the men and all the animals are called to stand near the ends of the plank. When one of the swinging beings falls down from the plank, the person standing near it will die sooner than the one standing at the opposite end. The deities have a messenger called Nutsɛkoa'lsika (that means "long ear"), who carries all the news from our earth up to the House of Myths. Aʟk'untä'm has two children, — the deer, who is called Snoȫ'lɛxɛlts Aʟk'untä'm, that is, "the foolish son of Aʟk'untä'm" (Plate VII, Fig. 8), and ʟĕɛxoniχ'is Aʟk'untä'm. I have not been able to learn any thing in regard to the functions of these two beings.

While Sɛnx and Aʟk'untä'm are principally concerned with the fates of mankind, they do not personally interfere with the doings of man. Their thoughts are carried out by four brothers, who are called collectively Masmasalä'nix or Ontsk·ĕ'mtɛnɛm (Plate VIII, Figs. 1–4). These brothers are Maʟapä'litsĕk· ("the one who finishes his work by chopping once"), Yula'-timot ("the one who finishes his work by rubbing once"), Maʟ·apĕ'exoĕk· ("the one who finishes his work by cutting once"), and ʟ·iʟn'lak·. They have a sister called ʟ·a'qumĕiks. These four brothers live in an elevated room in the rear of the House of Myths. They are engaged in carving and painting. It is said that they gave man his arts. They taught him to build canoes, to make boxes, to build houses, and to carve in wood and to paint. They taught him the methods of hunting, and, according to some, they made the fish. The Bella Coola say, when carving a design, that Masmasalā'nix gives them the idea which they are working out.

Senx has a daughter named Sp'ix·p'ik·ne'm, who invented the art of working cedar-bark. Her figure is also used in the kū'siut ceremonial, in which the invention of the preparation of cedar-bark is represented. This deity has an assistant called Omatōsē'k·, who supports the stick over the edge of which she is breaking the bark. When first breaking bark, she shouts, "Aлĕtx siāya'ltxau ti Omatōsē'k·stix" (" Bring to me Omatōsē'k·"). After he has been given to her, she shouts, "Aлĕtx siāya'ltxau ta tqɛnk·ʟts" (" Bring me the board on which to break the bark"). After receiving this, she demands the cedar-bark breaker, saying, "Aлĕtx snukpānʟai'ts ti sp'ē'k·tats." Finally she asks for cedar-bark, saying, "Aлĕtx k·ᵘʟōʟᴏlɛmx·laix· ti sp'ē'k·ĕtstēx·." Then she begins to work, singing,—

"E'sta aʟk·'x·auwē't ōʟ'ᴛnsʟ'ɛ msta la lau's
E'sta ntsanē'ts tsi Sp'ēx·p'ēk·inɛ'mtas Sɛnxalā'oɬa."

(" Behold me, ye who are not initiated!
I am the Cedar-bark Breaker of Sɛnxalā'oɬa.")

It seems that most of the Bella Coola maintain that the Raven also lives in the House of Myths, but this point of their mythology is somewhat obscure and contradictory. According to the tradition of a number of families, the Raven was one of the beings sent down by Senx to our world to become the ancestor of man, but at the same time it is told that he invented certain arts. It is stated that he made the first salmon-trap (aʟtk·u'l), which is used in connection with the salmon-weir.

It is also said that Masmasalā'nix attempted to make the whistles for the winter ceremonial, that he was unsuccessful, and that the Raven succeeded in making them; also that the Raven came down to give the world its present shape. He instituted the festivals of the Bella Coola, and then returned to the House of Myths.

Besides all these deities, there are nine brothers and their sister particularly concerned with the observations of the kū'siut ceremonial (Plate IX, Figs. 1–9). The names of the brothers are, Xēmxēmalā'oʟla, Xē'mtsiwa, Omq'ōmkī'lik·a, Q'ō'mtsiwa, Aimalā'ōʟela, Ai'umkī'lik·a, K·ᵘlē'lias, Q'ulaxā'wa, A't'māk·ᵘ; and of their sister, ʟ'ĕtsā'apleʟāna. These deities are painted with certain designs. Xēmxēmalā'oʟla and Xē'mtsiwa are painted with the designs of the full moon (the former carries a staff wound with red and white cedar-bark); Omq'ōmkī'lik·a and Q'ō'mtsiwa, with the design of the half-moon; Aimalā'ōʟela and Ai'umkī'lik·a, with the design representing the stars; K·ᵘlē'lias, with the design of the rainbow; Q'ulaxā'wa, with the design of the salmon-berry blossom; A't'mākᵘ has the shape of a kingfisher; and ʟ'ĕtsā'aplēʟāna is painted with the design of a sea-lion bladder filled with grease.   She wears rings of red and white cedar-bark.   The carving representing the kingfisher has the wings attached to the sides of the head, while the tail rises over the forehead.   Xĕmxĕmalā'oʟʟa is said to carry a small woman in his arms.   Her name is Nuspō'xta.   When the brothers and their sister threaten to do harm to man, she entreats them to desist.   In some traditions these deities are described as the children of Aʟk'untā'm.[1]

In one tradition ʟ'ĕtsā'aplēʟāna is described as visiting houses and stealing provisions.   She is then pursued by the person whom she has wronged, and returns to the House of Myths.   The deities are unable to cure her; but the person who wounded her is called in, and withdraws his arrow, whereupon she recovers.[1]   Formerly I had the impression that these ten deities were particularly concerned with the sisau'ḵ ceremonial,[2] but this impression has not been substantiated by the information I received during the past year.   The ten deities appear much rather as deities of the kū'siut.

In the rear of the House of Myths there is a room named ʟlō'sta, in which the son of the deities lives.   His name is Bā'ExōLla or SnupaaxoLa'lt.   When SEnx and Aʟk'untā'm desire to destroy their visitors, they send them past the door of Bā'ExōLla's room.   The latter then rushes out of his room and devours the visitors.   He also initiates the Cannibal.   According to the tradition of the tribe Sĕ'nxʟEmx·, they acquired membership in the Cannibal Society in the following manner: Bā'ExōLla came down to the mountain Sqtsʟ, where he met with the son of SEnxalō'ʟEla, the first of the tribe.   He conducted him up to the House of Myths.   He took him into his room, and gave him the name Q'oalaiu'tstimot.   He put a snake into his body, which enabled him to pass through the water.   When the youth applied his mouth to the body of a person, the snake tore pieces of flesh from the body, and devoured it.   Then Bā'ExōLla took the youth to the upper heaven, past the rent in the sky, and to the house of the supreme deity, Qamā'its.   The two approached the house, being blown towards it by the strong gale prevailing in the open country of the upper heaven.   They found Qamā'its sitting in front of her house; and she said to Bā'ExōLla, " Why don't you come in?   You wish that your friend should obtain great supernatural power.   Bring him to my house, and I will give him what you desire.   Stay for a short while where you are, and I will show you what I am doing.   Watch closely when the post of my house closes its eyes."   After a little while the post closed its eyes.   It grew dark at once, and the two visitors fainted, but soon they recovered.   When the post opened its eyes again, it grew light.   The visitors remained sitting on the ground, and

[1] Verhandlungen der Berliner Gesellschaft für Anthropologie, Ethnologie und Urgeschichte, 1894, p. 204.
[2] Seventh Report on the Northwestern Tribes of Canada, p. 6.

suddenly a strong wind began to blow, which rolled them over the prairie until they reached the door of the house. Then suddenly the wind calmed down. They remained sitting on the ground near the doorway ; and Qamā'its said, " Watch closely when the post of my house closes its eyes." They were sitting opposite each other, watching the post ; and when it closed its eyes, they were transformed into two stones, but they soon regained human shape. Then Qamā'its asked them to enter. Now the woman took the youth's blanket, and gave him another one made of bear-skin set with fringes of red cedar-bark. She told him that this blanket was to keep him warm, and that it would direct his course. Next she fetched some water from the salt-water pond behind her house. She sprinkled it over the faces of her visitors, and told the youth to sing about his experiences in the upper heaven when performing the Cannibal dance. If she had not sprinkled the faces of her visitors with water, they would have died. She said to the youth, " Your country is not far away. Do not be afraid of the dangerous road that you have to pass. Later on there shall be many Cannibals like you. Do not be afraid to touch the food that another Cannibal may offer to you. You are strong because you have seen me." Then Qamā'its sent him back to the lower sky. Here the gods placed him on the back of a bird (Sqᵘxsɛn), which carried him down to the sea. As soon as the bird reached the water, it uttered its cry, and at the same time the young man uttered the cry of the Cannibal. The people heard it, and said to one another, " That must be the boy whom we lost some time ago." They connected many canoes by means of planks, and paddled out to the place where the bird was swimming about. They covered the canoes with red cedar-bark and eagle-down, and tried to capture the youth ; but when they approached, the bird swam towards the village. They surrounded it with their canoes ; but the bird flew up, and disappeared in the sky, and at the same time the youth flew towards the village. When the people landed, he attacked them, taking hold of their arms ; and the snake, which was still in his body, tore pieces of flesh out of their arms. The people sang and beat time in order to appease him.

In a second room in the rear of the House of Myths, next to that of the Cannibal, lives Kōkō'sɛxɛm, another son of the deities. His room is called Nus'ō'lxsta. He initiates the Olx-dancer (see Chap. VI).

The path of the Sun is guarded by a number of deities. At sunrise is stationed the Bear of Heaven, Snanō's ti Sōnx· t'aix· (Plate X, Fig. 2). He is described as a fierce warrior, who protects the Sun against the attacks of his enemies, and he is the cause of the warlike spirit of man. His hair is tied up in a knot on top of his head. His mask is used in the sisau'k·

ceremonial, and sometimes in the kŭ'siut. The following song belongs to his mask and dance : —

Nanēmō'tstxuit ti q'oyaki'mtst'aix·. Nō̆ noq'awēxum ts'ɛn t'ayōLɛlat'aix· ayatɪ snanō's ti sōnx· t'aix·, wā, năn, ai!

("Cry now, as though you had left me! I shall tie up my hair, warriors, like the Bear of Heaven.")

At sunset stands an enormous post which is called Nutēexoa'axtatas ti Sōnx· t'aix·. It supports the sky, and prevents the Sun from falling down into the lower world. The trail of the Sun is described as a bridge which was built by Masmasalā'nix. The bridge is as broad as the distance between the winter solstice and the summer solstice. The Sun walks, his face turned towards the west. In summer he walks on the right-hand side of the bridge, in winter on the left-hand side of the bridge, which explains the varying heights of the sun in the course of the year. The extreme right and extreme left of the bridge are called Sē'ɛmt ("the place where he sits down," that is, the solstices). At each of these points a being is placed who is called Aʟk·x·ē'ʟnɛm (Plate X, Fig. 3). It is their duty to see that the Sun does not tarry too long at the solstice. If in summer or winter he should be inclined to stay too long or to return too soon, they regulate his course. When the Sun tarries too long at the winter solstice, the people say, "ēx tsēs pa'nia" ("salmon will be dried late this year"). If he leaves it without tarrying, they say, "ēk·!x· tsēs pa'nia" ("soon we shall dry salmon"). Three guardians named Naqumiqa'otsaix (Plate X, Fig. 1) accompany the Sun on his course, dancing around him all the time. The halo is called Itwu'xtsia ti Mānʟ t'aix· ("the cape of our father"). A sundog that appears westward from the Sun is called Aʟqōʟ ti Mānʟ t'aix· ("the painted face of our father"). The Bella Coola believe that when it drops down to our earth, it causes epidemics. During an eclipse the Sun is believed to lose his torch. The rays of the Sun are his eyelashes.

There are twenty-four guardians appointed to take care of the sky. They are called Nexolak·ai'x·. According to tradition, the sky must be continually fed with firewood. Once upon a time they put too much firewood into the sky and made it burst. All the pieces except one, called S'aʟwalō'sɛm, fell down to our earth. The fragments hit the faces of the twenty-four guardians, and distorted them. They tried to mend the sky, but did not know how to do it. They went down the river, and came to Masmasalā'nix, whose assistance they asked. Masmasalā'nix gathered up the broken pieces, and glued them together. Up to that time the Sun had staid in the east, but now he began to go on his daily course. At that time Masmasalā'nix built the bridge over which the Sun travels every day. He placed a wedge in the opening of the sky, into which the Nexolak·ai'x·

have to put the firewood. This opening is called Kˑawa′umsta, that is, "mouth kept open by means of a wedge." Masmasalá′nix spoke : "The sky shall not burst again. This wedge shall keep its mouth open." The following kū′sint song refers to these deities : —

Ai′mats tā mnatsai′ tūsxts ti sō′nxˑtsgˑi tˑaixˑ.
Aiělx tā mnatsai′ ōʟ ti Sˑaʟwalō′sɛms ti Sōnxˑ tˑaixˑ.
Skˑˑ yaˑlxˑtux ti si′lxnō tā mnatsai′.
Skˑa anōgˑa wa ɛxɛmě′x ti Kˑawa′umstaskˑ ti Sōnxˑ tˑaixˑ tā mnatsai′.

("My child perished like the sky when it broke.
Go to Sˑaʟwalō′sɛm of the sky, my child !
Gladden my heart, my child !
Sit down in the mouth of the sky, my child ! ")

Our world is called A′někō′ōʟ or Qɛnkˑi′lst, that is, "the land below." It is an island swimming in the boundless ocean. In the far east a giant is sitting with legs apart, who is called Aʟěp!álaxtnaixˑ. He holds a long stone bar in his outstretched hands. The earth is fastened to this stone bar by means of two stone ropes. Sometimes he gets tired, and moves his hands to take better hold of the stone bar. Then we have an earthquake ; and the Bella Coola say, "Sněnikᵘpstakˑīmtōʟs," that is, "he takes hold of our world." When he moves our earth westward, we have epidemics. When he moves it eastward, all sickness disappears.

In the ocean lives a being called Sɛʟsâts, who twice every day swallows the water of the sea and gives it forth again. This is the cause of the tides. A mask representing this being appears in the kū′sint ceremonial. He is represented as a human being, the face of which is painted with white stripes, which symbolize the various levels of the sea.

The world below us is the country of the ghosts (kōʟkᵘʟōlɛ′mxˑ). It is called Asiutā′nɛm. Descriptions of the ghosts' country are principally obtained from shamans who believe they have visited that country during a trance. According to the statement of an old woman who believed that as a little girl she had visited the country of the ghosts during a trance, the entrance to the country of the ghosts is through a hole situated in each house, between the doorway and the fireplace. The country of the ghosts stretches along the sandy banks of a large river. There is a hill behind their village, the base of which is covered with sharp stones. When it is summer here, it is winter there. When it is night here, it is day there. The ghosts do not walk on their feet, but on their heads. Their language is different from the one spoken on earth. The souls, on reaching the lower world, receive new names. The village of the ghosts is said to be surrounded by a fence. They have a dancing-house, in which they perform their ḳū'siut. It is just below the burial-place of each village. The dancing-house is very large and long. It has four fires. The women stay on the floor of the house, while the men sit on an elevated platform. The houses have doors, but the ghosts who first reach the lower world enter the house through the smoke-hole. A rope ladder placed in the smoke-hole facilitates their entrance. Two men stand at the foot of the ladder. They are called AnōeL'axsaLai'x. For a person who has once entered the dancing-house there is no return to our earth. The souls are at liberty to return to the lower heaven, which they reach by ascending the rope ladder. Those who return to the lower heaven are sent back to our earth by the deities, to be born as children in the same family to which they belonged. Those who enjoy life in the country of the ghosts, and who do not return to heaven, die a second death, and then sink to the second lower world, from which there is no return.

I received another description from an old man. He stated that he reached the country in his canoe. He saw two trails, — one the trail of the living, one that of the dead. He followed the trail of the dead, and reached a village in which there was a dancing-house. The language of the ghosts differed from that of the living (see p. 42).

The Bella Coola believe that in the far west is situated the land of the salmon, which is called Mia'ltoa. The salmon leave this country early in the spring every year, and ascend the rivers. They are believed to return to their own country in the fall. The following tradition is of importance, explaining the manner in which the salmon were first brought from their country to the rivers of our world : —

Once upon a time a man named Winwī'na lived at Q'ō'mqūtis. One day he was sitting in front of his house, looking at the river. He thought, "I wish fish would ascend this river." At that time not a single salmon visited Bella Coola River. Winwī'na entered his house and lay down, thinking about the salmon. One night while he was asleep he dreamt that with the help of all the animals he had made war upon the salmon, that he had vanquished them, and that since that time the salmon had ascended Bella Coola River. When he awoke he invited all the animals to his house, and told them about his dream. They all came, and when they had entered he shut the door. Then he spoke : "My brothers, I have invited you to my house that you may hear what I wish to do. You shall help me to obtain what I desire." The Mink asked him in what they were to assist him ; and he replied, "I want to go to Mia'ltoa. There is not a single fish in our river, and I dreamt that with your help I vanquished the fish. Let us make war upon them. I shall certainly take some slaves, and we will place them in this river." Mink retorted, "I am glad that you are speaking in regard to this matter. I asked my father the Sun (see Chap. V) to give us salmon, and I think he gave you the dream which you told us."

All the birds agreed, and they resolved to start as soon as possible. Then Winwi'na asked Masmasala'nix to build a canoe. The latter complied with his request, and made a self-moving canoe, to which he gave the names "Winaiötstuls" and "Kunkunu'qtstuls." In the third moon after the winter solstice the canoe was completed, and Winwi'na started, accompanied by the clouds, the birds, and by all the animals. The Hermaphrodite was sitting in the stern of the canoe. They went down the fiord; and when they passed the village of Bella Bella, they saw the Cormorant sitting on the beach, who asked to be taken along as a passenger. They travelled westward for a long time, and finally they reached the country of the Salmon. They saw that there were no trees. The country was a vast prairie. A large sun was shining in the sky. Soon they descried the village of the Salmon. They sent out the Raven as a spy. When he returned, he told them that in the evening the Salmon were in the habit of playing on the beach. Mink suggested that this would be the best time for carrying some of them away. Then the Crane (according to another version, the Hawk) said, "I shall carry away the Sockeye Salmon." The Wren said, "I shall carry away the Humpback Salmon." The Kingfisher (according to another version, the Crane) said, "I shall carry away the Dog Salmon." The Raven said, "I shall carry away the Silver Salmon." The Fish-Hawk said, "I shall carry away the Olachen and the Salmon Trout." The Cloud said, "I shall carry away the Spring Salmon." Finally the Cormorant said. "I am only a passenger, and I will take whatever I can get." The Mink remarked, "I will not say what I am going to carry away: I only want to tell you that you must each take one male and one female. Now start. You are invisible to the Salmon. When you approach them, they will not be able to see you, just as we cannot see the ghosts, even when they are walking by our side." They left Winwi'na to guard the canoe. Then all the birds and the Mink took each one male and one female child of the various kinds of fish. When they carried them off, the children fainted, as though their souls had been taken away. Their bodies remained at the place where they had been playing. The Salmon did not see their captors, and did not know why the children were fainting. The birds returned to the canoe, carrying the fish. Then Winwi'na said, "Let us go on and see what is beyond the country of the Salmon." Soon they arrived at a place called Qoalé'nia (this name is not quite certain), in which vast numbers of berries were growing. Here the Hermaphrodite went ashore, and picked all kinds of berries, which she carried into the canoe. Then they returned home. For seven months they had staid in the country of the Salmon. They reached the coast shortly after the winter solstice (?). When they passed Bella Bella, the Cormorant said, "This is my home. I will go ashore here." He went, and took along the Salmon which he had captured. Ever since that time there are salmon at Bella Bella. The others travelled on, and came to the mouth of Bella Coola River. Then they threw all the various kinds of fish into the water. The Salmon jumped, and began to ascend the river. Then Winwī'na arose in his canoe and told each at what season he was to arrive. He scattered the berries over the mountains and through the valleys, and told them at what season to ripen. After he had done so, he invited his companions into his house, and gave them a feast.

In this tradition the birds and animals are not called by their ordinary names, but by mythical names. These names are as follows:—

ENGLISH.	ORDINARY NAME.	MYTHICAL NAME.
Spring salmon	āmι̯	t'ōlt'ō'lx·timōt
Sockeye salmon	sāmι̯	nanūtak·anēExtɛnɛ'm ("very long")
Humpback salmon	k·ap'aī'	anuk·pɛmaī'x·
Dog salmon	t!li	siaia'ltoa ("fair weather")
Silver salmon	wa'is	k·!pstōstōsai'laix· ("making himself beautiful")
Salmon (sp. ?)	——	ō'sip'āq
Cloud	sk·!ē'noas	tsa koak· ("long hand")
Hawk (?)	stsix·ts'ɛx	anuk·!k·iqtsaix· ("looking down into water")
Wren	mōxat'a'laqa	ʟ'ik·ma'luʟaix· ("jumper")
Crane	xaq'ā'ns	masaxē'lian
Raven	qoa'x	ʟxoa'xoaqsai'laix· ("rising early")
Cormorant	ʟ'ō'pana	k·oā'k·oag·ila
Hermaphrodite	sx·inis	aʟa'ya'ō

According to the belief of the Bella Coola, Winwī'na's canoe arrives from the country of the Salmon every year. It stays in the country of the Bella Coola for nine months, and then returns to the country of the Salmon. At the moment when it leaves, another canoe, which is named "Nō'ak·nɛm" or "Nunuk·au'tsnɛm," which brings the kū'siut ceremonial, arrives from the country S'anōk!pta'ltua. The canoe reaches a distant point of land before the departure of the canoe of the Salmon. After four days it reaches a nearer point of land. Four days more, and it is seen at the point of land nearest to the mouth of Bella Coola River. Another four days, and it reaches the mouth of the river. The Indians believe that there is a house named Snō'amʟtɛnank· at this place. A post is standing in the water in front of the house. It is called Snutēxoalāaxtstɛna'nk·. In the house live three men who are named Naapsuʟaaxai'x·, A'mιtag·ilis, and Tix·ti·k·'ā'nɛmēm. The canoe is tied up in front of this house. As soon as it arrives, the kā'siut ceremonial begins. At the head-waters of Bella Coola River, forming the watershed between Bute Inlet and Bentinck Arm, is a mountain called

Smaya'na, that is considered a human being. It is said that his children make the canoe go up Bella Coola River with the rising tide, A'nxumk·ila. The canoe travels the distance from the mouth of the river to the mountain Smayá'na in a single tide. The canoe "Nō'ak·nEm" stays for four months. Then the canoe "Kunkunu'qtstuLs" returns from the country of the Salmon, while "Nō'ak·nEm" leaves again. It is said that all the gods of the House of Myths come to the villages of the Bella Coola in the canoe "Nō'ak·nEm."

The arrival and the departure of these canoes are strictly regulated according to the calendar of the Bella Coola, which for this reason should be explained in connection with their beliefs. The Bella Coola divide the year into two parts, which are separated by the winter and summer solstices. The solstices are periods of indefinite length, between which five months are counted. Each solstice is reckoned, therefore, as approximately six weeks. The names of the months are as follows : —

SēE'mt (*winter solstice*)	SēE'mt (*summer solstice*)
SxōLE'mx·EnEm	Si'Lxum
ALaō'nstimōt	Sexexē'mut
Siaq'u'm	SinuLlā'lsEmtEnEm
Sioiō'lx·	Tsi sitak·ā'ns tsEau Anaūlikuts'ai'x·
Sinō'moak·	LEmuLē'm

The canoe "Nō'ak·nEm" arrives, and "Kunkunu'qtstuLs" leaves, in the month SinuLlā'lsEmtEnEm. The canoe "Nō'ak·nEm" leaves, and "Kunkunu'qtstuLs" returns, in the month SxōLE'mx·EnEm.

At the moment when the canoe "Nō'ak·nEm" arrives, a deity called Anaūlikuts'ai'x· (Plate XII, Figs. 1 and 2), who is believed to live in a cave, opens the door of her abode. There is one deity of this name to each village. Her cave is called Nuskēsiū'tsta. It is said that one Anaūlikuts'ai'x· lives on the mountain Sqtsl.. Her house is described as a large hollow bowlder suspended from the top of the mountain by means of a rope. Each Anaūlikuts'ai'x· has an older sister who is called Nutsō'xEnEm. When the canoe "Nō'ak·nEm" appears, and she opens her door, she steps outside and stands in front of her house, dancing, with trembling hands. When a person sees her, he faints. His soul is taken into her house, and is initiated into the secrets of the kū'siut.

A particular Nuskēsiū'tsta is believed to be at the foot of the creek Anō'nk·, on the northern side of North Bentinck Arm, near the mouth of Bella Coola River. A woman called Nustsxoaxlō'stxuiL lives there. She is described as emaciated, of black skin, and as wearing a black blanket. A certain chief who lived long ago was the first to see her. He was initiated by her, and after his return he performed a dance, and told what he had seen. Then he died.

There is a special deity who initiates the shamans. His name is Laʟaiā'iʟ or Sxaî'êxoax (Plate XI, Fig. 9). He lives in the woods. He carries a wooden wand wound with red cedar-bark, which he swings in his hands, producing a singing noise. Around his neck he wears a large ring made of strips of bear-skin and red cedar-bark. He sometimes plays in ponds which are believed to be in certain mountains. When he jumps into the water, it boils. When a woman meets him, she begins to menstruate; when a man meets him, his nose begins to bleed. When initiating a person, he touches the chest of the latter with his wand, and paints his face with the design of the rainbow. Then he swings his wand, the noise of which causes the person who hears it to faint. He creates sexual desire in man and animals. A shaman who was initiated by this being told me that he very often sees Laʟaiā'iʟ, who tells him who will die and who will fall sick. Sometimes he sees that the body of a person is black. Others he sees dancing on their heads. These are signs that they will die at an early date. I obtained from this man the description of the visit to the country of the ghosts, quoted before (p. 38). He told me that when reaching the country of the dead, he saw the ghosts of his deceased relatives sitting in the house. When they saw him, they began to weep, and said, "Don't come here. We don't want to see you so soon." While they were speaking to him, the chief's speaker entered the house, and called all the people to come to the dancing-house of the ghosts. One of the ghosts painted his face black and white, and tied long strips of white and red cedar-bark in his hair. The people were called four times. Then they started to go to the dancing-house. The entrance to the door was over a narrow plank. When he had just stepped on the plank, he suddenly saw Laʟaiā'iʟ, with his large neck-ring made of red cedar-bark and strips of black bear-skin, who took hold of him, turned him round, and told him to return to his own country, because, if he should once enter the dancing-house, he would not be able to return. Then he revived; and from that time on, Laʟaiā'iʟ was his supernatural helper.

A. Jacobsen describes this spirit as follows :[1] —

"The most prominent among the spirits of the shamans is Kle-klati-e'îl [Laʟaiā'iʟ]. He lives in the woods, where the youth who intends to be initiated tries to find him. When the spirit meets him, the youth faints. When he recovers, he begins to sing a song, the tune and words of which have been given to him by the spirit. Now he has become a shaman, who uses this song in all his incantations; but he does not retain it throughout life, because he meets his guardian spirit almost every year, and then he receives new songs. The Indians believe that Kle-klati-e'îl has human shape, but he is clothed in cedar-bark, and wears a great many rings of cedar-bark.

---

[1] Verhandlungen der Berliner Gesellschaft für Anthropologie, Ethnologie und Urgeschichte, 1894, p. 104.

Some of these he gives to the shaman. . . . A third spirit is the Skaia [Sxai'êxoax], which is believed to live in rivers, and to have the shape of a salmon. When a shaman who is inspired by this spirit makes an incantation in a house, singing and dancing, as all the shamans do, whoever approaches the house and hears the song turns back. They believe that whoever passes the house during the incantation will be punished with death by the spirit Skaia."

I believe this spirit is identical with ʟaʟaiā'iʟ, who, as stated before, has the second name Sxai'êxoax. According to Jacobsen, some shamans are initiated by the ghosts. He says that the ghosts are believed to have bald heads and blue faces. I am under the impression, however, that the people initiated by them are not shamans, but kū'siut dancers (see Chap. VI).

Another being who initiates shamans is described in the following tradition : —

Once upon a time there was a man and a woman who had four sons. The three elder ones died. Then the father and mother and the youngest brother were very unhappy, and the old people cried for grief until they died. The young man was now left all alone. He left his village, intending to go away and never to return. He pulled his blanket over his head and walked on. Sometimes he would stop to pray. He lived on the meat of mountain-goats which he shot. He built a small hut high up on the mountains, and dried the meat. He was crying and praying all the time. He prayed to the Sun to give him a gift which would restore his happiness. One day early in the morning he ascended the mountain. He addressed the rising Sun, saying, " Look at me, how unhappy I am." After he had gone a short distance he came to a ravine. The bed of the ravine was filled with pretty pebbles. There he met a beautiful man, who was no other than the Sun, who had descended from the sky. He had caused the water of the creek that runs through the ravine to disappear. When the young man saw the stranger from a distance, he thought, " He seems to be looking for me." He went nearer ; and when they met, the Sun said, " I am the one to whom you are praying all the time, and I came to help you. Now be happy. When you open your mouth and speak to me, I know your thoughts at once. I help those who address themselves to me. Take this." With these words he handed the young man a switch carved in the shape of a man. The Sun was carrying it under his arm, the point of the switch directed downward. "Fold your arms and hold this switch to your chest, and then return to the village. When you approach any one, hide the switch under your arm. You will find a person who wears a nose-ornament of beautiful green color. Then you must try to hit the ornament with this switch, and throw it to your right side."

He walked on, and after a while he noticed a man sitting at a distance. Then he hid the switch under his arm. When he came near, he saw that the man wore a large green nose-ring. He hit it with his switch, and threw it to the right-hand side. Then the man said, "You have attained me as your supernatural helper. Your name shall be S'a'tᴇma [from 'a'tᴇma,' 'dead']. Many people have seen me, but nobody has done what you did. If you had not struck my nose-ornament, you would have died on seeing me. You shall have the power to heal the sick by the touch of your hands. Whenever a person dies and is put into a box, after the box has been placed in the burial-ground, go there. You will find me sitting on the coffin. If then you knock the nose-ring from out of my nose, I shall leave, and the dead will revive. He will break the box, and will arise."

Then the young man felt very glad. He returned to the village, and by following the instructions of the spirit he resuscitated the dead. He was given many blankets, and the men whom he had resuscitated gave him their daughters in marriage.

Other shamans are initiated by ᴌ'ëtsä'aplᴇᴌána. The same man who gave me the record of his supposed visit to the country of the ghosts (see p. 38) told me that at another time he saw ᴌ'ëtsä'aplᴇᴌána flying in the air outside of his house. She wore a ring of red cedar-bark around her neck. She was turning round all the time. Songs were coming from all parts of her body. Although she did not open her mouth, it sounded as though a great many people were singing. She gave him a song, or, as the narrator expressed it, "she threw a song into his body." At that time he was sick, suffering from a wound in his leg inflicted by an axe. He said four days after meeting the spirit he was able to walk, and since that time she has assisted him in curing diseases.

The si'siuᴌ is another helper of the shaman, and the means of curing disease (see p. 28). It appears that it obtains its supernatural power from the fact that it lives in the water in which the supreme deity washes her face. When a person sees a si'siuᴌ, he should throw sand on it, by which means he will be able to catch it. Its skin is so hard that it cannot be pierced with a spear or knife. The person who catches it should not try to cut it with his knife, but should stretch his hand backward, and thus he will find the leaf of a holly, which is the only thing that can cut its skin. He should not touch the si'siuᴌ with his hands, but hold it with hemlock twigs. He should wrap it in white cedar-bark and tie it up in his blanket. If it is not thus tied up, it will disappear. It must not be taken into the house, but should be placed in a small box and hidden under stones, or buried in a hole under the root of a tree. It is a most potent means of curing disease. Sick people will buy small pieces of the si'siuᴌ, for which they pay high prices. The piece is thrown into water, in which it is kept for four days. Then the water is used for washing the body. If a healthy person uses this water, he will live to an old age. Sick persons chew the white cedar-bark in which it is wrapped up, in order to regain health. They must not swallow the cedar-bark, but only the saliva that gathers in their mouths. A person who has chewed the cedar-bark becomes invulnerable. The eye of the sī'sinᴌ is described as about a foot in diameter, and as transparent as rock crystal.

Toā'laᴌ'it is the spirit who protects the mountain-goat hunter. He himself is invisible; but great hunters sometimes see his hat, his moccasins, or his mountain staff moving about. The following tradition describes some of his characteristics:—

The Raven and the Lynx lived in one house, each occupying one side. Early in the morning the Raven went out to catch salmon with the harpoon. He was very successful, and carried the fish home. Toā'laᴌ'it watched the Raven, who, when he arrived at the house, roasted his salmon. The children of the Lynx were sitting near by, and looking at the Raven while he was roasting the fish. They wished to participate in the meal, but he did not give them anything. Then the children were very sad. Now the Lynx made up his mind to make arrows and to go hunting mountain-goat. He went out and cut some wood for his arrows; then he told his wife to make a quiver, which he called Tsō'lapᴇla. She did so, and wove a quiver of cedar-bark. The Lynx was quite impatient for the sun to rise, so eager was he to start hunting. Early in the morning he arose and ascended the mountain. When he reached the limit of the trees, he sat down on a flat rock and looked for goats. Then he saw the staff of a man who was coming down the mountain. He did not see the person himself. He thought, "Who is that? Who may be hunting here?" The stick approached him; and when it came near, he saw Toā'laᴌ'it, who wore a large hat. His hat was named Q!pōᴌ (that means a "barren mountain-top"). Toā'laᴌ'it reached the Lynx, and sat down opposite him. Neither spoke a word. After a while Toā'laᴌ'it arose, took the arrows of the Lynx, and said, "How beautiful these arrows are!" He took up one after another until he had looked at all the four arrows of the Lynx. Then he asked, "Who made these arrows?" The Lynx did not reply. Toā'laᴌ'it asked again, "Who made these arrows?" Then Lynx replied, "Toā'laᴌ'it made my arrows." Then Toā'laᴌ'it was very much pleased, and said, "Is he the one who made your arrows?"—"Certainly," replied Lynx. Then Toā'laᴌ'it took his arrows and threw one after another down the mountain, and said to the Lynx, "Now go down the mountain and look at your arrows. If you spoke the truth, every one of them will have killed a large mountain-goat." The Lynx descended the mountain, and saw that every one of his arrows had killed a goat. Then he was glad, because now he had food for his children. He jumped and danced for joy. And Toá'lau̯'it said, "I am Toá'lau̯'it. I am so called because I am the mountain-goat hunter. Now return to your village. From now on, I am your supernatural protector. The next time you go hunting, and you do not find any mountain-goats, sit down and throw your arrows down the mountain. Every one will kill a goat. But do not lose those arrows. If you should lose them, you would never kill another mountain-goat." The mountain-goats were so large, that Lynx took only their fat, which he put into his quiver and climbed down the mountain. He arrived at his house in the afternoon. He left his quiver outside, and the Raven saw him coming in. The Lynx sat down by the side of his wife. He did not say a word. His wife and his children also received him in silence. In the evening, when it was dark, he said to his wife, "Go and fetch my quiver. It is hanging outside on a stick." She went there and tried to lift it, but it was too heavy. She returned to her husband and told him that she was not strong enough to lift it, and asked him to fetch it himself. He said, "It is not heavy." He went out himself and brought it in. He opened it and took out the fat ; and he gave some of it to his children, but he did not give any to the Raven's children. Then the Raven was very sad. After a little while, the Raven's children began to cry, because they wanted some of the fat.

Early the next morning the Lynx went to fetch the meat of the mountain-goat. The Raven watched him, and saw where he went. When he saw that the Lynx had killed mountain-goats, he made up his mind to go hunting too. He told his wife to make him a quiver while he went out to cut wood for his arrows. In the evening the quiver and the arrows were done. In the afternoon the Lynx came home, bringing the meat of the mountain-goats. Early the next morning the Raven started, following the tracks of the Lynx. He reached the place where the Lynx had sat down. He sat there, and placed his arrows by his side. He looked around for mountain-goats. After some time he saw a staff moving along in the distance. It approached, and soon he saw a man coming down the mountain. It was Toá'lau̯'it. He reached him, and sat down opposite the Raven. They did not speak a word. After a while Toá'lau̯'it arose, took up the arrows, and said, "Man, your arrows are beautiful. Who made them?" The Raven did not reply. Then Toá'lau̯'it said again, "Tell me who made your arrows." Then the Raven answered, "The name of the man who makes my arrows is Raven." Then Toá'lau̯'it took the arrows, threw them down the mountain, and said to the Raven, "You are bad!" And he turned back, and ascended the mountain. The Raven went down the mountain, trying to find his arrows.

They had hit a stone, and their points were broken. He staid there some time, and when it was nearly dark he returned home. Before he reached his house, he cut his own belly and took out some of the fat from his intestines. He cut it in five pieces, and replaced his intestines. He put the fat into his quiver. When he reached his house, he hung the quiver up outside, and entered. He imitated everything the Lynx had done. When it grew dark, he told his wife to fetch his quiver. She brought it, and he told her to open it and to feed his children. She took the fat out, placed it on a stick, and put it near the fire; and as soon as it grew warm, the Raven cried, "Tttt! Don't put it so near the fire. I feel sick when you do so." He jumped up, took hold of the fat, and put it back in his belly. The Lynx said, "Formerly I fed your children, but you were the first not to treat me properly. You did not give any food to my children." Then the Lynx took some fat, and flung one piece to each of the Raven's children. He cut some meat and gave it to them also. Then the Raven said, "I will give you one of my children, that it may grow up in company with yours."

It is said that the former spirit Toā'laʟ'it was killed at one time by an Indian who took his place. This tale is recorded in Chap. IV. It belongs to the tribe of the village Nusxē'q!. A similar tradition is told of Astas,[1] by which name the Carriers call the Raven, their principal culture hero. Many traditions referring to Astas are common to the Carriers, the Bella Coola, and the Awī'k'ēnôx of Rivers Inlet.

The Bella Coola believe that a being called Kᵘtsōs is the father of all mountain-goats. When a hunter meets him, he thinks he sees a kid. Then he should close his eyes and open them again. If the animal is Kᵘtsōs, it will appear in its real shape as a buck of enormous size. The hunter should then ascend the mountain. If he should descend, he would fall and die.

The thunder-storm is produced by the Thunder-bird, who lives on the mountains, in the company of a number of spirits, who are considered his particular friends. The Thunder-bird himself is represented by a black mask with red nostrils. The nose is strongly curved, the forehead bulges forward, and the chin protrudes almost as far forward as the nose (Plate XI, Fig. 1). His herald is called Aʟxulā'tɛnum (Plate XI, Fig. 2). His face is painted with orange and blue stripes, and he carries a speaker's staff, which is painted with spirals of the same color. He watches the door of the Thunder-bird's house. In his house live the Rabbit (Plate XI, Fig. 3); the Owl, who is considered the rival of the Thunder-bird (Plate XI, Fig. 4); the Mountain, ʟ.ō'qoᵗs (Plate XI, Fig. 5); the Raindrop (Plate XI, Fig. 6).

[1] Verhandlungen der Berliner Gesellschaft für Anthropologie, Ethnologie und Urgeschichte, 1894, p. 300.

The Thunder-bird and his companions appear in the kū'siut ceremonial. When they enter the house, a dancer appears who carries an instrument in the shape of a bird-rattle (Plate XI, Fig. 7), which is provided with holes in its lower side, and has a loose back. This implement is filled with cedar-bark and eagle-down, and is shaken by the dancer. The eagle-down is thus made to fly about in the house, symbolizing the wealth and power of the Thunder-bird.

IV.

In the preceding pages I have summarized the principal features of Bella Coola mythology, which are characteristic of the traditions of the whole tribe. Besides these, there are other groups of traditions which are very conflicting. One reason for the existence of numerous contradictory traditions must be looked for in the peculiar social organization of the Bella Coola. In former times, when the tribe was populous, the Bella Coola inhabited a great many villages. The inhabitants of each village are considered the descendants of a number of mythical ancestors who were sent down by Sᴇɴx. Each of these village communities has traditions of its own, which are its property, and which are not well known to the rest of the tribe. Many of these traditions refer to the origin of our world, and for this reason a number of the most important myths differ in various villages. Indications of such conflicting ideas may be found in the traditions recorded in the preceding pages. To make this subject clear, it is necessary to describe somewhat fully the traditions belonging to a number of village communities. Before recording these traditions I shall enumerate the villages of the tribe. The following list is the result of repeated inquiries. In it the names and locations of the villages are given in consecutive order from the mouth of Bentinck Arm upward along Bella Coola River, and the names of the mythical ancestors of the village communities have been added where these have been ascertained.

VILLAGE.	LOCATION.	ANCESTORS.
1. Q'oā'ʟɴa	At the bay of this name.	
2. Sᴇ'ʟia	At the entrance of South Bentinck Arm.	Tōtosō'ɴx.
3. Nusxē'q!	On North Bentinck Arm.	Sᴇmsintā'k·as, Nusqoa'-xʟɪnē, Sx·ints, and their sister Ē'ɴʟ'aʟana.
4. Pē'isʟʟa	At the entrance of the valley opening on the north side of the mouth of Bella Coola River.	Stā'ltomx· Yuyō'lkᵘ, Mᴇntsi't, Sisiū'ʟ.
5. Aʟqla'xʟ	The present mission at the north side of Bella Coola River, near its mouth.	Isyā'yōt, Xēmxē'mtᴇ-ɴᴇm, Sɴuxɴaʟa'ls, and their sister Nuqai'tsta

VILLAGE.	LOCATION.	ANCESTORS.
6. Osmaxmik·e̍'ɬp	North side, at mouth of Bella Coola River, above No. 5.	
7. Txe'ix tskunē	North side, at mouth of Bella Coola River, above No. 6.	
8. Selku'ta	North side, at mouth of Bella Coola River, above No. 7.	
9. Sa'qta	North side, at mouth of Bella Coola River, above No. 8.	
10. Stsk·ē'iɬ	South side, near mouth of Bella Coola River.	Q'ēe̍'t.
11. Q'ō'mqūtis	South side, near mouth of Bella Coola River, above No. 10.	Xē'mlaix·, O'mq'ōmki-lik·'a, and their sister Sxemā'na.
	(Nos. 4–11 jointly are called Nuxa'lk·!.)	
12. Sēnxl	About one mile above Nuxa'lk·!.	Yuyō'lkumai, Anuxe'm-laix·, Senxalō'oɬla, and their sister Nusk·i̍'m-naɬ.
13. Tsomō'oɬ	On Bella Coola River, above No. 12	Nō'ak·ila, Tsxlemɬma-k·ai'x·, and their sister Snutk·'ana'ls.
14. Snū't'ɛle	On Bella Coola River, above No. 13.	ɬuk·lai'x·.
15. Nūk·i̍'ts	On Bella Coola River, above No. 14.	ɬxumtɛne'm.
16. Nusā'tsɛm	At junction of Nusā'tsɛm and Bella Coola Rivers.	Qxōxunk·ma'nē.
17. Asɛ'nənē	On Bella Coola River, above No. 15.	Ē'mask·in or Aɬq'ēexa'.
18. Nuqā'axmats	On Bella Coola River, above No. 17.	Anutapak ɛmɬai'x·, Is-yū'vot, one more man, and their sister.
19. Tsxoaxqā'nē	On Bella Coola River, above No. 18.	
20. Nūsq!ɛ'lst	On Bella Coola River, at foot of Mount Nūsq!ɛ'lst, above No. 19.	Totō'sk·ma.
21. Nuɬɬe̍'ix	On Bella Coola River, above No. 20.	Sxumxumlai'x·, Sō'nx-mai, Sinoxi̍'aɬ, and their sister Qanāatsla'qs.
22. Stū'ix·	28 miles above mouth of Bella Coola River, above No. 21.	Aɬɬix·'imōt sis ti Sōnx t'aix·, Sexē'm, Xē'm-tsioa Anuxē'm, Kès-mi̍'o, Nutseqō'ax, and their sister Kēmiowa'-na.
23. Snū'ɬ'ɛlaɬ	On Bella Coola River, above No. 22.	
24. Siɬ'ax·	On Bella Coola River, above No. 23.	
25. Q'oa'px	At head of South Bentinck Arm.	
26. Nū'iku	" " " "	
27. Asē'ix	" " " "	
	(Nos. 25–27 jointly are called Tā'lio.)	
28. Sōtsɬ	At mouth of Salmon River, Dean Inlet.	
29. Sātsq	Dean Inlet.	

It is very remarkabl   that, besides the ancestors of the villages enumerated here, the Bella Coola state that the Sun created a number of men
when he sent down to a mountain on Skeena River, and that they became
the ancestors of a part of the Tsimshian. Another group of men was sent
down to Bute Inlet, and later on migrated to Bella Coola River. The names
of these villages and men are as follows : —

VILLAGE.	ANCESTORS.
Nusqa′pts (Skeena River)	Teqō′mnōɪ, A′ustē, Sxō′ya, and their sister Kˑ′imiɪqa′n.
Na′as (Bute Inlet)	Nānatskuit, Anoxēma′axots, Spä′n-paɪɪnaix·, O′meaɪkˑas.

The full traditions referring to them will be found at the end of this
chapter. Each of these ancestors, when sent down to our world, received a
salmon-weir, which was placed across the river at the locality where the
built their village. I shall now relate a number of traditions of the variou.
villages.

TRADITION OF SE′LIA.

In the beginning our world was dark. At that time Tōtosō′nx descended
from heaven, and reached our world on a mountain near the river Wa′k·i-
tɛmai (Fraser River). Here he built a house, in which he lived in the
company of the Raven. The latter had a black canoe which was called
" Raven." The two resolved to travel in order to find people. They descended the river until they came to the sea. After some time they reached
a house which was covered inside and outside with abelone shells. The
totem-post of the house was also covered with shells. It shone like the
sun. They saw a canoe on the beach, and this too was completely covered
with abelone shells. A chief, whose name was Pɛlxanē′mx· ("abelone man"),
invited them to enter his house. As soon as Tōtosō′nx reached this place, the
sun rose. If he had not found the place of the abelone chief, there would
be no sun. Tōtosō′nx did not wish to stay. He looked at the house, and
saw something turning about on top of it. When they came nearer, he saw
that it was a Mink, which was running about on the roof. Many people
were inside the house. When Tōtosō′nx approached and saw the beautiful
canoe, he wished to have it. He offered the chief their canoe in exchange.
This offer was accepted, and Tōtosō′nx travelled on with the abelone
canoe. The Raven staid with the abelone chief. Tōtosō′nx continued his
travels, following the course of the sun. First he travelled southward,
and came to the post which stands in the west of our world. From
here he travelled on, and reached the copper country, which is situated

a little farther to the north. When he saw the country from a distance, it looked like fire. When he came near, he saw a house which was built of copper. On the beach there was a canoe, which was also made of copper. The chief was sitting in front of the house, and invited him to come in. A carved post in the shape of a man was standing in front of the chief's house. It also was made of copper. Then Tōtosō'nx offered to exchange canoes with the chief. The chief took the abalone canoe, while Tōtosō'nx took the copper canoe. The chief also gave him a large box made of copper, and he gave him his daughter ᴌa'liayᴕts in marriage. Besides this, he gave him olachen, which was to serve as food for his daughter. In the copper box were all the whistles and other paraphernalia of the sisau'k· ceremonial. He travelled on, and reached our country in the north. When he arrived, the sun began to shine for the first time. He met a chief, to whom he gave the sisau'k· whistles. Wherever he met people, he presented to them the whistles of this ceremonial. Thus he met the Haida, the Tsimshian, the Git·amā't, the Gitlō'p, the Xa'exaês, the Hĕ'iltsuq.

He travelled on, and reached Wa'nuk (Rivers Inlet). There he threw the olachen into the water. They multiplied, and since that time there have been many olachen in that river. He travelled on, and came to Nux·ī'ts, to Sō'mxōᴌ, and to Ts'ī'o, on the lake above Rivers Inlet. He gave the chiefs of these places the sisau'k· whistles. He arrived at Asĕ'ix, in Talio'mx·. Here he left whistles and olachen. He did the same at Q'oa'px and Nū'ikᵘ! in South Bentinck Arm. Then he travelled down the fiord to the little island Qe'nk·ilst, at the mouth of South Bentinck Arm. Here he left the sisau'k· whistles. Finally he came to Sᴇ'ᴌia, near the entrance to South Bentinck Arm. He liked this place very much, and was surprised not to see any people. He travelled on, and reached the mouth of Bella Coola River. Here he staid four winters. He used his whistles, and performed the sisau'k· ceremonial. At the end of this time a quarrel arose between him and the chief at Bella Coola, therefore he turned back. When he came to Sᴇ'ᴌia, he stopped and built a house. The house resembled in shape that of the chief ᴌa'lia. He called the house "ᴌa'lia." His wife, the daughter of the chief of the copper country, had many children. They increased rapidly, and became the tribe Sᴇᴌia'mx·. He invited the neighboring tribes to a feast. He performed the sisau'k· ceremonial. He never gave feasts in honor of his youngest son, Sᴇ'nxag·ila.

Sᴇ'nxag·ila was dissatisfied with the way in which his father treated him. He went to bed, and for four days could not be induced to rise. On the fifth day he rose early in the morning and left his father's house. He lay down on a point of land, crying. There he staid all day. For four days he staid at this place. At midnight he returned home and lay down in his bed. He would not be induced to come down to the fire in the middle of the house. His mother said to her husband, "Do you know what ails our son?" After four days he left the house again, and lay down on the point of land. Here he fell asleep. Suddenly, at midnight, he felt somebody shaking him, saying, "Arise! I am going to give you supernatural gifts." When he looked up, he saw a young Seal standing beside him. The youth arose. When he looked up again, he saw the Seal's house on the water. It had risen from the bottom of the sea. The house was full of loons, one of which was sitting on a pole in front of the house, crying continually. Sᴇ'nxag̣ila and the Seal entered, and inside there was a large fire. It was as bright as though the sun were shining from out of the water. They approached the house. In front of the door was a monster, Kʻi'lxʻta (Plate XI, Fig. 8). At the threshold was the monster Skʻamtskʻ. Sᴇ'nxag̣ila and the Seal entered the house through the roof, thus avoiding these dangerous creatures. Q'ōmō'qoa,[1] who wore a hat of enormous size, was sitting inside. He was the chief of the house. In the right-hand rear corner of the house he saw two men sitting. The name of one of them was Nunuxēmalslai'xʻ. Another man was sitting in the left-hand rear corner, beating the drum. His name was Bᴇ'lquit. Two others were blowing whistles. They were performing the sisau'kʻ ceremonial.

Now, Sᴇ'nxag̣ila had seen the whole house. It had become his supernatural property. He left it, and the house disappeared under the water. Then he returned home, and told his father what he had seen. He ordered his father to sweep his house, and to strew it with new sand. He invited all the neighboring tribes in, and distributed a great many presents. After the festival, Sᴇ'nxag̣ila built a house like the one he had seen on the water, and he took the name Axʻaxsmō'sᴇm ("the one who invites"). His house was painted with designs of waves, gulls, loons, and of the monsters Skʻamtskʻ and Kʻi'lxʻta. When dancing, he wore a cap made of loon-skins.

Fillip Jacobsen records another version of this tradition.[2] He calls Tōtosō'nx "Wakilmaj," which is evidently a misprint for "Wakitmai," which is the name of Fraser River, where, according to my version, Tōtosō'nx descended from heaven. Wakitmai is a word borrowed from the Kwakiutl language, meaning "the greatest river." Following is a brief abstract of this version of the tradition : —

Wakitmai (Tōtosō'nx), Omkil (O'mgʻilis?), Kamokija (Q'ō'moqoya), and Kvassina (Qoatsi'nas), and their sisters Litsemkil (Lē'tsumgʻila?) and Kolil, descended in the shape of ravens from heaven to Bella Coola. At that time there was no daylight with the exception of about one hour every

[1] Masks representing this being and his wife have been figured in Internationales Archiv für Ethnographie, Vol. III, Plate III, Figs. 1 and 2. The specimens in question are in the American Museum of Natural History (Cat. Nos. 16/1504 and 16/1505).
[2] Ymer, 1895, pp. 1, ff.

day, and the sea extended far up Bella Coola valley. At their request, Masmasalā'nix made a self-moving canoe for them, which was called "Koo-koo." They travelled to Fraser River, and then continued their journey southeastward, accompanied by their speaker. After some time they reached the house of Pelkhanny (Pᴇlxanē'mxˑ). They were invited in, and received as a gift the secrets of the sisan'kˑ dance and some mother-of-pearl. (There is no mention of the appearance of the sun.) After four days they continued their journey, and reached the house of Klallia (ʟa'lia), the chief of the coppers, from whom they received other secrets of the sisau'kˑ and some copper. On returning, they reached Rivers Inlet, and on a small island met an old woman who was twisting branches from a tree. When she looked at their canoe, her eyes assumed the peculiar lustre of mother-of-pearl. The woman was the crab, whose eyes still retain this lustre. Her answers to their questions showed them that they had been absent many years, although they thought their journey had lasted not more than four days. They dragged their canoe from the head of Rivers Inlet to the lake above, thus creating the river which empties into Rivers Inlet. Sea-lions and whales ascended through this river into the lake. Wakitmai transformed the whales into stone. He threw his canoe-pole at the sea-lions, intending to drive them back. He missed them, and the pole stuck in the mountain. It may still be seen there. For this reason the mountain is called Skallakt (Skōlō'kˑʟ), which means "canoe-pole." He had also received a magic wand from the chief of mother-of-pearl, one end of which possessed the power of restoring life, while a touch of the other end caused death. By means of this wand he transformed the sea-lions into driftwood. The brothers continued their journey to Tallio (Tā'lio), where they met a family. Then the brothers separated, and Wakitmai settled at Bella Coola. He married the daughter of the couple whom he had met at Tallio. He had a son and a daughter, who grew up in four days. Then Wakitmai initiated them into the sisau'kˑ ceremonial which he had received. He went up to Alkondam (Aʟk'untā'm), from whom he received further instructions. One of his sisau'kˑ masks represented himself in the form of a raven; the other one, the chief of the mother-of-pearl.

TRADITION OF NUSXᴇ·Q!.

The Sun sent down Sᴇmsiutā'kˑas, Nusqoa'xlanē, their sister E'nʟ'aʟana ("darkness"), and the Hermaphrodite (Plate XI, Fig. 10) to Nusxē'q!, which is situated on Bentinck Arm. The Sun desired that two Bears should assume human shape and live with them, but his wishes were not realized; only their eyebrows assumed the shape of human eyebrows. These two Bears were living at Mo'asla'ʟ. There is a cascade at this place, at the foot of which they caught salmon. The Bears obtained there all the food they needed. One day SEmsiutā'k·as went down the river to see the sea. He was sitting near the mouth of the river, and then the Sun sent the olachen to the river. The Hermaphrodite was the first to see them, and began at once catching fish. If he had not done so, there would have been a great many olachen in this river. But women are forbidden to catch them, therefore the Sun grew angry, and took away the greater number of the fish. Instead of them, he sent cohoes salmon. When SEmsiutā'k·as reached the sea, he took the name Nŏnotxoq!E'maix·. He went across to ALqla'xL and married Nuqai'tsta, the daughter of Isyū'yŏt. On the following day she had a child, which after four days had grown to be a youth. His name was Xĕ'mak·sta. Then they all went back to Nusxē'q!. When they reached there, the boy wished to go up the river. He carried his bow and bird-arrows along. When he had gone some distance, he met some people who wore ornaments made of red cedar-bark and bear-skins. The youth saw them, and they approached him. They invited him to follow them to their house. They were Bears, although they looked like men. When they had entered the house, the Bears invited the youth to sit down. They started a fire by striking together two green stones. Then they said, "We will roast some salmon." They took some skunk-cabbage and roasted it ; and when it was done, they placed it in a dish and gave it to the boy. When the boy began to eat, he found that what appeared to be skunk-cabbage was really salmon. Their dish was made of the knee-pan of a Bear. The youth thought that the food they gave him would not be sufficient to still his hunger. The Bears knew his thoughts at once, and said, "You will not be able to eat all that we have given you." The young man began to eat, but he was unable to empty the dish. When he had eaten, he took a drink of water ; and the Bears finished the dish, and placed four berries (st!Els) in it. Again the youth thought, "That is not enough for me ;" and the Bears knew his thoughts at once. When the youth took up a berry and began to eat, he saw that another one had taken its place, and he was not able to empty the dish. After he had eaten, he wished to return home. But the Bears said, "Stay here. You may return to-morrow." The Bears showed him to a bed on one side of the house, while he himself lay down on the opposite side.

Early the next morning the Bears said, "Now let us start. We will take you home." But the one night that he had staid at the Bears' house was actually a year. The youth was carrying his bow, and the Bears wished to have it : the youth gave it to them. Then one of the Bears stretched his hand backward in his bed, and took out a beautiful staff made of crystal. He said, "If you want to heal a sick person, touch him with this end of the staff ; but if you want to kill your enemies, point the other end at them, and they will die. This shall be your supernatural power." Once more the Bear stretched his hand backward in his bed, and took out some eagle-down, which he gave to the youth; and he gave him a bear-skin blanket and said, "If any one should maltreat you when you return home, take this down, put it on your left shoulder, and shake it. Then it will fly up, and when it settles on his skin, he will fall sick. Then, if you wish to cure him, approach him with the healing end of your staff, and he will recover." The Bears gave him the name Stsk·!la, and said, "When you arrive at the house of your parents, do not enter at the door. Stay behind the house. Soon somebody will come, and then you may show yourself. And when they find you, tell them to open the rear of the house. There you shall enter, and you shall sleep in the elevated room in the rear of the house." The Bears accompanied him until they were near the village. Then they returned. The youth staid behind the village.

Soon he heard his mother crying in her house. Then he approached cautiously, and knocked on the wall close to the place where she was sitting; but she only cried the louder. She thought that the people were teasing her. Again he knocked on the wall. Then the woman wiped her face and stopped crying. She told her youngest son to see who was knocking on the wall of the house. He ran out and soon returned, saying, "My brother is standing outside." Then she struck him with a stick, saying, "Why do you say that? He died long ago." Then she said to her older son, "Go out and see who is knocking on the wall." Soon he returned, saying, "My younger brother spoke the truth. Our elder brother has returned, but he does not want us to come to meet him. He wants father to open the rear of the house." This was done, and an elevated room in the rear of the house was prepared. Xĕ′mak·sta entered, and staid in the room for three nights. His youngest brother always staid with him.

On the fourth evening he said to his youngest brother, "To-morrow I shall go to Nuxa′lk·. I wish to see my relatives. But I shall soon return. Do not be sad because I am going to leave." Then he walked along the north side of the fiord, over the mountains. He came to a house at Aʟxla′xʟ. He saw a man sitting behind the house, and addressed him, saying, "Tell my relatives that I wish to see them. Let the young women come out here." The man entered the house, and soon returned, leading two women. When they reached the place where Xĕ′mak·sta was standing, he said, "Sit down. You shall see who I am. Look at me well. Now I shall stand over there." Then he took his staff and pointed its deadly end towards the women. They fell down dead. While they were lying there, he touched their bodies with his hands. Then he turned his staff, pointed it at them, and they arose. Now they loved the young man because he had resuscitated them, and they wished to marry him. The young man stepped behind their backs, went round them, and when he came in sight again he had assumed the shape of a bear. His body was covered with red cedar-bark. Then the women were afraid. He went round them, passing behind their backs, and when he re-appeared in front, he had re-assumed his human shape. Then he put some eagle-down on his left shoulder, and approached them. He shook himself, and the down fell on them. At once their skin became covered with sores, and their bodies inflated. He went round them once more, and healed them by means of his staff. When they had recovered, they were highly pleased with the great powers of the young man. Then he said to them, "Now return to your houses." They went, but very soon they began to long for the young man. They returned and lay down with him. Then he sent them back home and asked them to return in the evening.

He sent his friend to bring other women, whom he seduced in the same manner. He had all the young women of the village visit him. They all bore children to him. After all the women on the north side of the river had visited him, he swam across and did the same to the women on the south side of the river. When the people learned what he was doing, they resolved to go to his house and kill his mother. The young man who had led the women to Xĕ'mak·sta heard about it, and told his friend what he had learned. He said, "The people intend to kill your mother because they think you will be sad when you hear about her death. They are furious because you have seduced their daughters and wives."

Now the people prepared their canoes, and started early in the morning. They took along all their canoes, in order to prevent Xĕ'mak·sta from following them. Xĕ'mak·sta said to his friend, "Tell me when they start, but do not say any thing about my plans. Look and see if you can not find an old broken canoe that has been placed over the salmon-weir." The young man said there was a canoe of that kind. Xĕ'mak·sta instructed him to wait until the people had left, and then to take the canoe down and place it in the water. He also told him to wait for him at K·tsō, at the mouth of Bella Coola River. The young man did as he was bidden. As soon as he placed the canoe in the water, it was whole like a new canoe. He landed at K·tsō, where he was met by Xĕ'mak·sta, who jumped into the canoe, shook himself, and assumed the shape of a bear. Xĕ'mak·sta went up and down the canoe once, and then he resumed the shape of a man. He said to his friend, "Let us go to Anu'sx on the north side of the fiord." There they landed. Then he said, "Now I shall run home over the mountains. Watch me as I run along, and follow slowly in your canoe. You will see what will happen to the people." At that time the trees on the mountains were small. When they were near the shore, Xĕ'mak·sta turned round and assumed the shape of a bear. Then he ran over the mountains, and reached his home long before the people were able to get there. He entered his father's house and told those within that the people of Nuxa'lk· were coming, intending to kill his mother because their daughters were all in love with him; but he promised to vanquish his enemies without any assistance. Now the canoes were approaching. Then he sent his speaker to the beach, and told him to warn the enemies. When they were within hearing distance, he shouted, "Do not come ashore! The shaman is here and will kill you." The people laughed, and said, "How is that possible? He is in our village."—"You lie!" replied the speaker. "He is here." But they did not believe him. They ranged themselves in a row, waiting for the tide to carry them in. At high water the signal was given to land, and then all paddled for the shore. Then Xē'mak·sta took his bear-skin blanket and covered it with down. He stood on the roof of his house and shook himself. The down flew about and settled on the canoes, and all the people fell sick. They groaned with pain, and their skin became sore and swollen. Then he entered the house and called his father and his friends. The speaker shouted, "Did I not tell you not to come here?" The enemies were unable to propel their canoes, and were groaning with pain. After a few hours the youth said to his mother, "Now watch me. I am going to cure them." He took his staff, and pointed the healing end in the direction of the canoes. Then all the people recovered. The down flew back to him, and he hid it. When they had recovered, they shouted, and threatened to kill the youth and his mother. They landed, and were about to enter the house, when he pointed the deadly end of his staff at them. They fell down dead. Only one of the people who had staid in the canoe remained alive. After a few hours the youth said to his father, "Now I will resuscitate them." He touched the chief of Qō'mqutis with the end of his staff, and he arose. Now the chief offered the young man his daughter in marriage, and asked him to resuscitate the other people too. The youth did so, and the people arose, rubbing their eyes as though they had slept. And every one whom he resuscitated requested him to restore his friends to life too, and they gave him their daughters in marriage.

Semsiută'k·as's son had four boys. These young men went up the river to hunt mountain-goats. They pitched camp, and then they separated, and each went to a different creek. Early in the morning they ascended the mountain, and three of the brothers returned in the evening loaded with game. But one of the brothers did not return. The other brothers grew anxious, and when he did not return on the evening of the following day, one of them went out to search for him. He followed his tracks, but did not find him. The two remaining brothers waited a long time, but neither of the other brothers re-appeared. After two days the third brother went out. He said to the youngest brother, "Please stay here. I must go and find my brothers." The young man waited, but his brothers did not return. Two days after the third brother had started, the youngest one left the camp to go in search of his brothers; but he did not follow the trail his brothers had taken. After a while he saw smoke far away in the distance. He thought, "Maybe my brothers are staying there." He went near, and saw a house. He looked in at the door. He saw a woman standing in the house, who had her blanket tied around her waist. She was dressing a large skin which was stretched over a frame. The young man thought, "I will go and touch her genitalia." He entered, and when she bent down, scraping the skin, he touched her. The woman was frightened. She looked back and saw him. She was very beautiful. Her name was Almenmena'm. She talked to the young man, and asked him to lie down with her. He complied. Then she set before him a dish filled with meat of the mountain-goat, and she said, "Do not eat too much. My husband will be here soon, and he will try to offer food to you, but do not be afraid. I shall assist you. Take care that you do not fall asleep. He will come back late in the evening, and he will give you much to eat in order to make you sleepy. Take this bag and hide it under your blanket, and when my husband turns his back, slip the food into it. He wants to see you eat all he gives you." And she continued, "After he has fed you, he will tell you to lie down to sleep. Then, when you hear my husband saying, 'Hwu, hm!' imitate his sounds. If you should not reply, he will take his staff and he will point it at you, and you will be dead. He always ties his dogs to the bed-post. If you succeed in killing my husband, you may marry me."

After a while the man came in. The woman saw his staff far away. He was carrying two mountain-goats which he had tied to his belt. The man was no other than Toā'laL'it. Now he came in and said to his wife, "Somebody has been to see you." He sat down and said, "A man is here. He slept with you, therefore you did not tell me." — "Yes," she replied, "it is true." Then Toā'laL'it made no further remark. After a while he ordered his wife to build a large fire. He intended to cook the meat, and to set it before the visitor. He carved one of his mountain-goats, and he ordered his wife to heat stones in the fire. Then they roasted the neck of the goat on the spit, and Toā'laL'it cut the fat and put it in a dish. Then he set it before the man. Toā'laL'it watched to see if he was eating. The man tried to leave a part of the food in the dish; but Toā'laL'it went up to him and said, "Why do you eat so slowly? See how fast I am eating!" And he devoured a large dish full of meat very rapidly. He swallowed it without chewing. Toā'laL'it next took the fat of the mountain-goat and placed it in a dish, which he gave to the young man. He emptied it into his bag. Next he gave him a piece of the brisket; and when Toā'laL'it turned away, he hid it in the bag. Toā'laL'it was watching him all the time, but every now and then his wife spoke to him in order to induce him to look in another direction. Now they had finished eating. Then Toā'laʟ'it showed the young man the place where he was to lie down. He told him to go to sleep quickly, because he himself was very tired too. He said to him, "Do not trouble to arrange your bed. You are too tired." Then he led his two dogs to his own bed, and tied them to a post. His dogs were wolves. He tied one to each side. Now Toā'laʟ'it lay down, and soon he shouted, "Ee!" As soon as he had done so, the young man answered in the same manner. After a while, Toā'laʟ'it uttered the same cry, and the young man replied. When it was almost daybreak, the young man heard Toā'laʟ'it snoring. He shouted, "Ee!" three times, but Toā'laʟ'it did not reply. Then the woman whispered to him, "Arise! Take his staff and point it at him." The young man did as he was bidden. As soon as he pointed the staff towards Toā'laʟ'it, the latter died. The woman ordered the young man to free the dogs. As soon as he had untied them, they bit off the head of their former master. The young man had vanquished him.

Next to Toā'laʟ'it's house there was a deep precipice. The woman said to the young man, "Throw Toā'laʟ'it's body down this precipice." While he was doing so, he looked down and saw his lost brothers lying in the abyss. If the youngest one had not touched the woman, he would have died too. Then the woman said, "Now your name is Toā'laʟ'it, and these dogs shall be your dogs, and this staff shall be your staff, and this quiver shall be your quiver." And when it grew day the woman said to him, "Ascend the mountain and sit down there. When you see a goat, shoot it with one of your four arrows. If your aim should not be true, your arrows will turn and hit it, anyway. When you go hunting on the mountains and do not see any goats, take your staff and point, and for each time you point you will have a goat. And take my dead husband's hat and his blanket and his belt. You must not carry the goats on your back. Carry them at your belt, one on each side. You will be able to carry them be they never so heavy." On the following day the man started. He killed a large goat and hung it on his belt. Soon he returned home. Then the woman said, "Now you are just like Toā'laʟ'it. You must sleep with me for four nights, and four nights leave me alone." And she said, "If you see any one who wants to have goats, and feels very unhappy, you shall help him. You shall meet him, and he will find many goats."

Tradition of Alqʟā'xʟ.

Isyū'yōt, Xēmxē'mtɛnɛm, Snuxnaʟa'ls, and their sister Nuqai'tsta, were sent down to the mountain Sqtsʟ. Xēmxē'mtɛnɛm had a son who was called Aʟtsī'ax. Their house was called Nuqoaxō'ts wa tkʟa'nats. That means "the raven box." The posts inside the house represent men. The front is painted with the design of a raven. They are the ancestors of the Aʟqlaʼxʟ. It is said that Nuqaiʼtsta married the son of Sᴇmsintaʼk·as, the ancestor of the tribe of Nusxēʼq!.

Tradition of Stsk·ēʼʟ.

Alk·ʼalaʼlis, with his three brothers, was sent down from heaven to the mountain Skolōʼk·ʟ. They descended the mountain and settled in Stskʼēʼʟ. Here they were visited by the Raven and his tribe. They saw that the people of the Raven had an abundance of abelone shells, while they themselves did not possess any. Then Alk·ʼalaʼlis said to his brothers, " Let us try to find abelone shells." They covered the bottom of their canoe with mats, launched it, went aboard, and started. Whenever they met any one, they hid on the beach. Finally they reached the ocean; and after they had travelled a long time without finding abelone shells, they intended to return, but they had lost their way. When they turned their canoe to go back, they seemed to be surrounded by land on all sides. They did not know which way to turn, and began to cry. Night came on; and when it grew daylight again, they saw a Raven soaring over the canoe. He came down lower and lower, and finally lighted on the canoe. He said to them, " My name is Qaʼʼxaxsila. I am going to give you supernatural power. I shall show you the way you desire to go. You will find a cave in yonder mountain. Cover your canoe with mats, and enter it." They did as they were bidden. They found that the roof of the cave was covered with starfishes, which fell down on their canoe, but they were kept from them by the mats with which they were covered.

After some time they emerged into the open. They found themselves near a beach which was covered with abelone shells. They filled their canoe, and covered their paddles and their hats with shells. Then Alk·ʼalaʼlis's brother took the name Winx·sĭʼwala, his second brother took the name Nuswēʼnɔmx·, and the third one took the name Satĭ!ĭʼla. Now they were glad, and they prepared to return to their home. The Raven, who had staid with them, gave them directions which way to go. They returned after a year's absence. When they were approaching their village, Alk·ʼalaʼlis said to his youngest brother, to tease him, " I am sure only your wife has remained true to you; but our wives, I think, have given us up for lost, and have taken new husbands. When the brothers arrived home, they found that only Satĭ!ĭʼla's wife had remained true to her husband. All the others had taken new husbands. Then the elder brothers were ashamed. They showed the people their canoe filled with abelone shells. They married again; and Alk·ʼalaʼlis had a daughter, to whom he gave the name Aʟpʟʟxaʼnyuʟēʼx.

Later on he had another daughter, whom he called A'tsta. Then he took the name Ix·ialxōtsai'x·. He called his house T!a'palst, and the painting on the front of it represents a canoe called "T!kun."[1]

The tradition of the ancestors of the village Stsk·ē'iʟ is not quite certain. Besides the preceding legend, I received the following one: Isyā'yōt, Xē'mtsiwa, Xēmxēmalā'oʟʟa, and two women, Lētxumlaix·aia'na and AʟQ'ēxayana, were sent down to Skōlō'k·ʟ. Before they left heaven, Masmasalā'nix had given them the olachen. They also carried the nusxē'mta, the box in which the daylight was kept. Their speaker was Emtɛnk·ai'x·. He caused the olachen to disappear, and later on to re-appear. It is also said that when they came down from heaven a cold wind was blowing down the mountain Skōlō'k·ʟ. Then the Raven took his canoe-pole, and pushed it upward towards the mountain, thus causing the wind to stop. For this reason the mountain has its name, which means "canoe-pole."

There is still another tradition referring to the origin of the tribe of Stsk·ē'iʟ. The Sun made one man whom he called Q'ēēt and Eq'ōʟa'm, and he made another man whom he named Aqla'm. He gave to Q'ēēt the skin of the bird Qō'xōx, which is sitting on the post of the House of Myths for use in his dances. For four days these men sat at the foot of the pole. Then they descended to our earth, carrying the nusxē'mta, which gave them light on their way downward. They reached the mountain Skōlō'k·ʟ, whence they descended to Stsk·ē'iʟ. Here they built a house. Q'ēēt saw a man sitting in front of a house which was built of branches. His name was Qoa'lsanʟ. Q'ēēt married his daughter. He visited many villages, where he married the daughters of the chiefs. Therefore he had relatives in a good many places. He married at Nuqa'axmats, Snā't'ɛle, Nuk·ī'ts, Asɛ'nanē, Nūsq!ɛ'lst, Nuʟʟē'ix, Stā'ix·, Q'oā'ʟna, Bella Bella, and Rivers Inlet. All his wives gave him their houses. Then he returned to his own country, while he left his children with their mothers. He had two men who were guarding the entrance to his house. Their names were Qôiotsī'tas and Naamtōtsai'x·.

TRADITION OF NUSĒ'ÊX.

The Sun sent two Ravens, and their sister the Crow, down to ʟxtsāētx (Gitamat). They carried the nusxē'mta, in which the sun was kept. The Raven asked his younger brother to break the nusxē'mta; but the latter refused, requesting his elder brother to do so himself. Then the elder Raven broke it. After he had thus liberated the sun, he took the name Kumkunɛ'm. His brother took the name Xēmlai'x·. Then their sister told

[1] This is also the name of Qamā its's canoe (see p. 28).

them to leave the country, and to seek a new home. Kunkune'm went to Sātsq, where he built a house near a lake. There he caught beavers and other animals; but he desired to find people, and descended towards the sea. When he reached the fiord, he met an eagle with human face, whose name was Qoa'sta. He asked him, "How long have you been here?" And he replied, "I have been here a long time. I am older than you." He proceeded down Deans Inlet. He met a bird named ALmEnā'm, and he asked, "How long have you been here?" He also replied, "I have been here a long time, I am older than you." His people, the SūtsLE'mx, were the saw-bill ducks. KunkunE'm asked the bird for a canoe, that he might proceed down the fiord. Then the bird made a canoe for him, burning out a cedar-tree. He gave him a double-bladed paddle. Finally he reached Nusē'ex, on the south side of Bella Coola River, near its mouth. Here he built a house. Then a woman named ALExma'na came down to this place. Her blanket was set with small coppers, which made a noise whenever she moved. She told him to place a copper in front of his house. He met two women named Xēmlaix·'a'na and Xē'mtsiwa in Stsk·ē'iL. He called all these women his sisters. KunkunE'm's brother and sister settled in Sātsq.

TRADITION OF SENXL.

Yuyō'lkumai and Qoa'x were sent down by the Sun to the top of the mountain SqtsL. The Sun said to Yuyō'lkumai, "You shall give to the tribes their languages, and you shall live in SENXL." When Yuyō'lkumai came down with his sister, Nusk·i'mnaL, the Sun gave him the names AnuxÉ'mlaix· and SEnxalō'oLla.[1] Qoa'x was very sad, and was sitting quite still on the top of the mountain SqtsL. He did not like the earth, and wished to return to the sky. He had lost his fire-drill. Then he assumed the shape of a deer, and ran up the mountain, and while there he found the fire-drill and took it back. At that time there were no trees on the ground, only small herbs. Yuyō'lkumai took leaves and made a small hut just large enough to sit in. He lay down to sleep. Very early the next morning he arose and looked outside. Then he saw a large salmon-weir in front of his hut. The Sun said to Yuyō'lkumai, "Lie down on the top beam of the salmon-weir, and look into the water. I am going to place a stick in the water as long as a cubit. I shall put on it four abelone shells. If you should not find it in the water to-morrow morning, you may conclude that there are no people like yourself in the world." He did not see the stick on the following morning, and concluded that there were no people living higher up the river.

_____

[1] Another time I understood that these were three men and one woman.

At that time the Sun did not shine very brightly, and the Raven thought, "I will ascend the river to find a better Sun." He did so, and after travelling a long time he came to a house called Kowā'msta¹. He entered, and saw the sun-box hanging from the roof of the house. He cut the rope by which the sun-box was suspended, and carried the box away. As soon as he touched the box, the present Sun came out of it. Then the Raven returned, and he sang a sisau'k· song, telling how he liberated the Sun. He took the name Kımkung'm. He travelled on, and came to the house of Yuyō'lkumai, to whom he gave his new name and his sisau'k· song. Then the people were very glad that they had a good Sun.

Yuyō'lkumai was very sad because he had no house. The Sun knew his thoughts. One evening he lay down to sleep. Early the next morning he arose and stood near his salmon-weir. When he looked at the middle of the river, he saw a bright light. It was the Sun, who had come down the river. He beckoned to Yuyō'lkumai, who went to meet him. Then the Sun asked, "Why are you sad? To-morrow morning you shall see a house like the one you desire to have. Do not think you are poor. I am going to give you everything you desire. To-morrow morning you shall see a new house standing right here. It will be your property."

When Yuyō'lkumai awoke next morning, he looked around, and saw the house standing there. It was close to the salmon-weir. The front was painted with the design of the Sun. He entered the house and sat down, and thought, "What shall I eat in my new house?" The Sun heard his thoughts. When it grew dark, and no food had come to him, he lay down and was very sad. On the next morning, when he awoke, he heard people singing near his salmon-weir; and when the Sun arose, he saw a large canoe tied up at the post of the weir. It was filled with provisions. There were fish of all kinds, and berries. It was the canoe "Nō'ak·nem" or "Nunuk·au'tsnem"² ("bringing food"), and the occupants of the boat gave him the song and dance sqoɔ'lxoalem, and they gave him the name Xĕ'mtsioa.

TRADITION OF NUK·I'TS.

Lxumtenē'm was sent down by the Sun to Snukʼɔsikʼɔ'ol. He became the ancestor of the Nuk·I'ts. He acquired the giant Qoatiwa'la as his super-natural helper. The house of the giant was full of copper plates, which sounded every morning. He left his house every morning and travelled all over the world, carrying away to his house women from all the villages. Then he married them. He gave his copper plates to Lxumtenē'm, who then

---

¹ Compare K·awa'umsta ("open mouth of sky;" literally, "mouth kept open by means of a wedge"), p. 36.
² The canoe that brings the ku·siut (see p. 40).

took the names ALix·lixuma'k· and Anuk·ĭ'ts'ɛm. His last name means
"whirlpool," signifying that his house swallows wealth as a whirlpool swallows
whatever comes near it.

Tradition of Nusq!e'lst.

Totŏ'sk·ma was sent down to the mountain Nusq!ɛ'lst, where he built a
lodge of caribou-skins. He took the name Xĕmxĕmalá'ᴏʟla. At that time
the Raven was travelling all over the world in order to see if salmon were
living in all the rivers. He met Totŏ'sk·ma, and said to him, "There shall
always be salmon in the river Sa'sʟmet."

Tradition of Nuʟʟē'ix.

The Sun sent Sxumxumlai'x·, Sŏ'nxmai, Sinoxi'aʟ and their sister Qanāatsla'qs down from heaven. They were the first Nuʟʟē'ix. They reached
the earth on Mount Setsk·aiix. They brought a salmon-weir with them.
They lived in an underground lodge, the entrance to which was in the middle of the roof, the floor being reached by a ladder. The woman had a child
who was continually crying. One day, while she was holding the child in
her arms, she looked up and saw looking down the entrance-hole a person
whose throat and face were perfectly white. She nudged her husband, and
called his attention to the person. He looked up, and knew at once that it
was the Snĕnē'iq. He took his bow and arrows, but he did not rise. Then
he spanned the bow, shot, and hit the Snĕnē'iq right in the throat. The latter
rolled down the roof of the house. Early in the morning the man arose,
climbed the ladder, and saw the Snĕnē'iq lying dead in the grass, his face
turned upward.

The old Snĕnē'iq lived in the mountains. When her son did not return,
she set out to search for him. She did not find any trace of his body, and
she gave him up for lost. Just below Stū'ix· she sat down on a flat rock,
crying bitterly. She cried, "O-unuu!" Her cries were so loud that they
were heard far away. Four strong men set out to see who was crying. They
saw her from a distance, and did not dare to ascend the river any farther.
They were afraid of her. When they returned and told that they had seen the
Snĕnē'iq sitting on the bank of the river, all the people were afraid. They did
not know what to do. There was one man living in the village who did not
participate in their discussion. While all the others were expressing their
fears, he did not say a word. Early the next morning he put a mat in his
canoe, launched it, and went up the river with his steersman. He was not
afraid. When he reached the place where the Snĕnē'iq was sitting, he
stopped on the bank of the river just opposite her. Then the young man

told his companion that he was going to cross the river to see the Snēnē'iq from near by. He did so, and when he reached her, he touched her feet, and joined in her wails. After a short time she stopped. Then the young man said, " I came here because I am your friend." And she replied, "I lost my child, therefore I sit here wailing." Then she arose, took a copper on which she had been sitting, and said, " My dear, you pitied me, therefore I will give you supernatural powers. I will be your supernatural helper. Look at my house. It is very large, and beautifully painted. When you build a house, decorate it in the same manner, and every thing I have here shall be yours. You shall distribute it among your people. I am now going to Na'us."

The young man returned home, carrying the copper in his mat. He told his friends what had happened. Upon his request, they accompanied him to the house of the Snēnē'iq, and helped him to carry down the presents which he had received. Then the young man gave a festival, and distributed the presents among his tribe.

TRADITION OF STU'ÎX·.

The Sun sent down ALli'x·imōt sîs ti Sōnx t'aix·, Sēxē'm, Xē'mtsioa, Anuxē'm, Kêsmï'o, Nutseqō'ax, and a woman, Kêmiowa'na, from Nusma'ta. They came down at a place near sunrise called ALtitxā'axLElxs ti Sōnx t'aix·. In their house all the languages were written down, and were distributed among the various tribes. Nutseqō'ax did not assume human shape, but remained what he had been in heaven, a wolf. They began to travel down Bella Coola River. Anuxē'm staid at Kōlnalōs, near the source of Bella Coola River. Kêsmï'o staid in the country now inhabited by the T!aa'nsnē (" Carriers "). The others went down towards the sea over the mountains. Sēxē'm carried their house in a small box. Its name was Nuts'axma'ls. Finally they arrived on Mount Nū'ya. That means " bare mountain." They descended to the river, and put down the house, and it enlarged until it reached the natural size of a house. A horse-fly was painted around the door, and on each side a sun was represented.

TRADITION OF SOTSL.

The Sun sent Isyū'yōt and Xē'mtsiwa down to the mountain Suwa'k·x·, near Nū'ɪ.!ɛl. Their sister, who came down with them, was named Qa'qma. Xē'mtsiwa and Isyū'yōt wore eagle blankets. When they left the mountain Suwa'k·x·, Isyū'yōt said to his brother, " Let us make canoes. If you should finish yours first, come to visit me. If I should finish mine first, I will come to see you." Then Isyū'yŏt went down the mountain and settled on the north side of Bella Coola River, at the foot of Mount Sqtsʟ, where he built a house. He was the first to finish his canoe, and started to go to Nū'ʟ!El. He came to Snuqʟi'tq, a small river on North Bentinck Arm, where he erected a post. He went on, and came to Q'a'nuk which is opposite to Snuqʟi'tq. He went on, and came to Snŏskᵘ!ʟ, Sxwaxuē'lk·, Stsqoa'sma, Anuʟxum, K·ā'p'ai, and Ts'ē'xŏts. In all these places he erected posts. Then he saw his brother, who was sitting on a log, wrapped in his blanket. First he thought that he was an eagle, but soon he recognized him. He thought, "Didn't he assume human shape? Did he retain the shape of an eagle, which he had in heaven?" Xĕ'mtsiwa was looking at the river all the time. When Isyū'yŏt reached him, he said, "Didn't you assume the shape of a man?" His brother replied, "No, I could not do so, because this place is too dangerous. I brought down the olachen, but it cannot go up this river." Isyū'yŏt retorted, "I have taken possession of a great many places. I erected posts wherever I went." Then Xĕ'mtsiwa said, "That is not right. You ought to take possession of one place only, of the one where you built your first house. Now look at my country." Then Isyū'yŏt saw that the river was disappearing under the mountain Snwa'k·x·, that it was impossible to ascend it in canoes, and that no fish was in the river. Then Isyū'yŏt said, "Let us call some people, in order to make this country inhabitable." Then both arose, and considered what to do.

At this time Noak·ī'la, with his brother Ts·a'k·us and his sister Sʟ·ax·ʟ·axta'aʟ, came down from heaven. They came out of the hole in heaven, and intended to descend the river to Nū'ʟ!El; but Noak·ī'la found that the river was exceedingly dangerous, and they did not know how to proceed. Then he called Masmasalā'nix. He wanted him to make a canoe. Masmasalā'nix came down to his assistance, and made a canoe, which he called "Qoaqoā'usalŏʟ." When they reached the place named A'sk·lta, Noak·ī'la's brother and sister landed. They became the ancestors of the tribe of that place. Noak·ī'la himself proceeded down the river, and came to the place where it disappeared under the mountain Snwa'k·x·. Then he asked Masmasalā'nix to break the mountain, in order to open a way for the river. The brothers Masmasalā'nix tried to split the mountain by means of wedges, but they were unable to do so. Then Noak·ī'la called the hauhau. It came, and pecked the mountain with its beak, intending to break it, but it did not succeed. Then he called the xtsaltsalŏ'sEm, which is also called sī'siuʟ,[1] a snake which lives on the mountains. It crawled about on the mountain Snwa'k·x·; and where it crawled the mountain split in two, making

---

[1] The sī'siuʟ is described as similar to a fish. It has only one head; while among the Kwakiutl it is represented as having one head at each end, and one in the middle. The Bella Coola say that when first seen it is very small, but becomes larger and larger when being looked at (see also pp. 28, 44).

a passage for the waters of the river. Then Noak·í'la descended the river and met Xĕ'mtsiwa. Now Xĕ'mtsiwa was happy, because a way had been opened for the river. He threw " his eagle dress, and became a man. Isyū'yōt returned to Nuxa'lk·.   descendants use the eagle mask and the eagle blanket.

TRADITION OF SĀTSQ.

In Sātsq lived the chief, Smawu'n, who had descended from heaven to the mountain Yūlyulɛ'ml. The name of his youngest son was Aʟ'ōsqɛmnai'x·. This young man had a son, whose name was Sŏ'nxuak·as. He wished his son to marry, but the latter refused to do so. Often his father invited girls to the house, but he refused them, and sent them back to their parents. Finally his father grew angry, and said to him, "Leave my house, if you do not want to marry, and go wherever you please." Then the boy became sad. He went into his room and lay down. He staid in bed for four days, because the words of his father had hurt him. Then he arose and ascended the mountain behind the house. After travelling a long time, he came to a river. He followed the course of the river downward. After some time he heard a noise like that produced by the striking-together of two sticks. He crept up cautiously to discover its cause. When he came near enough, he saw a log lying on the ground, which was turning all the time, but he saw no living being near by. He also saw an axe chopping it, as though a man were building a canoe, but he did not see any one. He saw the canoe being finished with marvellous rapidity, and then moving towards the water. It was sliding over a number of sticks that were lying on the ground, but he did not see any one placing the sticks under the canoe. The young man followed the canoe cautiously. Now it reached the water. He looked down the river, and some distance away he saw houses from which smoke was rising. The canoe went down towards the smoke, and landed. Then he saw four men come out of the houses, launch a canoe, and go up the river. They went past him up the river. When they had reached a place a little above him on the opposite side, they started to cross; and he thought, "It looks as though they were coming to see me." Soon the canoe landed, and one of the men said to him, "Come aboard. We have known for a long time that you were coming to pay us a visit." He accepted the invitation, and they returned to the village. The name of the chief of the village was Ha'mts'it, one of the ancestors of the Gitlop. Masmasalā'nix had been making a canoe for him, but had remained invisible to the young man. They went down the river Sxstswax. They landed near the village; and when they entered the house, the young man was told to sit down on the right-hand side of the fire. They gave him to eat; and after he had finished eating, the chief arose, took his four daughters, and placed them opposite the young man, on the left-hand side of the fire. Then the chief said, "I knew that you were going to visit me, and that you left your home because your father scolded you. Here are my daughters. Point out the one whom you wish to marry." He selected the second one. Her room was in the rear of the house. The front of the room was painted with the design of a whale. Then the chief sent his daughters back into their rooms. He said, "If you had selected my oldest daughter, I should have given you all my traditions; but since you selected the second one, I am going to give you part only. Now return to your father, and tell him to come to fetch my daughter."

The young man returned, and after a day's journey reached his father's house. After he had staid there one day, his father and his tribe went to fetch the girl. They carried much property, which they intended to give to Chief Ha'mts'it. When they arrived at the village, they staid outside the house, and the chief told his family tradition, as is the custom among the Bella Coola. Then they were married.

While they were sitting in the house feasting, they heard whistles in one of the rooms. After a while the sound stopped. Then Ha'mts'it said, "Now you observe that I am a true chief. These whistles belong to me. I give you this box containing my dance ornaments, the whale painting, and the whistles. Don't be afraid to sound the whistles. Use them during the sisau'k⋅. I am the only one who uses whistles in the sisau'k⋅. You are using whistles in the kū'siut, but not in the sisau'k⋅." Then he gave him one side of the river, so that the middle line formed the boundary between his own country and that of the young man. Then he filled with grease a large ladle, which was carved in the shape of a raven, and gave it to the chief. He said, "Heretofore I used this spoon in my feasts, but now it belongs to you."

They staid there for four days, but the girl did not come out of her room. On the fifth day Ha'mts'it sent them back. Then they prepared their canoes, and Ha'mts'it brought the girl out of her room. She carried four small stones. Ha'mts'it said, "I want my daughter to have two of these stones on each foot. They shall be her slaves, and they shall assist her when she distributes property."[1] Then they returned to their own village, and the young man built a large house.

TRADITION OF ANOTHER VILLAGE.

The Sun sent down an eagle named Anutapak⋅ɛmalai'x⋅ to Mount Ts'ɛlk⋅t ("eagle"). With him came Isyū'yōt, one other man, and one woman whose name I have not been able to learn. The eagle took the

---

[1] It seems that these stones were intended to symbolize female slaves, each stone representing a slave.

name Sikulkultsŏ't, and built a house. Before he came down from heaven, he wrote down the languages of all the different tribes, the cries of the animals, and the songs of the birds, and distributed them. He had a child whose hair was as white as an eagle's head.

Tradition of Nusqa'pts.

The Sun sent down Tēqō'mnōᴌ, A'ustē, Sxō'ya, and their sister K·imiᴌqa'n. Tēqō'mnōᴌ did not want to go to Bella Coola. He preferred to go to Nusqa'pts, which is situated on Skeena River. Therefore the Sun took him down to that place. The Nusma'mt (the Tsimshian) saw the place Nusqa'pts, which is situated on a small lake, and desired to have it for their own use. Then Tēqō'mnōᴌ became angry, and fought with the Tsimshian. They killed Tēqō'mnōᴌ's brothers. Only Tēqō'mnōᴌ himself and his sister K·imiᴌqa'n were saved. They were very sad, and went up the River Nusqa'pts to return to the Sun. While Tēqō'mnōᴌ was walking up the river, he met a Bear, who said to his sister K·imiᴌqa'n, "I want to marry you." — "No," she said, "I do not want to marry. If I should lie down with you, I should always be thinking of my brothers." They came to the source of the river. They saw a person approaching from a distance, and soon they recognized the Sun. He asked, "Why did you come here? Are you unhappy?" — "Yes," replied K·imiᴌqa'n. "My brothers have been killed, and therefore I came up the river to see you." Then the Sun said, "We will go up to heaven." He took her up and married her. The next morning the woman had a son, who was called Sqōᴌ ("wasp"). It grew night, and it grew day again; and the boy had grown very much, so that he was quite tall. Then the Sun said to his wife, "I want you to return with your son. If the people want to attack you again, tell the boy to use this bow, and let him shoot upward, making a chain of arrows which will reach downward from the sky."

Then K·imiᴌqa'n and her son returned to the earth. One morning the boy went out to play with the other children of the village in which they were living. Some of the children pushed him, and the boy said, "Don't do that, else my father will be angry. He told me so." Then the children laughed, and said, "Who is your father?" Sqōᴌ replied, "The Sun is my father." One of his playfellows retorted, "How is it that your father is so beautiful and you are so ugly?" and they all maltreated him. He cried, and went back to his mother's house. He said, "I am going to shoot my arrows toward the sky, that my father may know how the people have maltreated me." Early the next morning he took his bow and shot an arrow towards the sky. It stuck there. Then he shot another one, which hit the notch of the first arrow. Thus he continued until he had made a chain of arrows.

Then he climbed up to the sky, went to his father, and said, " My play-fellows maltreated me." After he had reached his father's house, he gathered up his arrows. The Sun said to his son, " To-morrow I shall punish those who maltreated you." Then he stretched his eyelashes down to K·iniɪ.qa'n's house, and told his boy to descend along them. Early the next morning the Sun looked at the house of the people who had maltreated the boy. Then he wiped his forehead, and the perspiration fell upon the house. It caught fire at once. The floor of the house became red-hot, and the people rushed outside. They jumped into the water, but the water began to boil. Only K·iniɪ.qa'n's house did not burn. She stepped out of the door, looked at the people, and said, " I am glad to see that you are being punished." The people perished in the water of the lake. Then the Sun wiped his face again, and the fire ceased to burn. Now the people who had escaped knew that the boy was the Sun's son. They treated him kindly, and since that time they have increased in number.

Tradition of Na'us.

Anoxema'axōts, Spanpaɪɪnai'x·, O"meaɪk·as, O"meaɪmai, and Nana'tskuiɪ. were sent down to Na'us. They desired to move to Nuxa'lk·!, and travelled overland until they reached the mountain Nusq!e'lst, where they found stones for making axes. At that time the bird Qlē'lx·'ana was living on Nusq!e'lst. He was frightened away by the arrival of Anoxema'axōts and his brothers, and went to Mount Smayā'na, which is between the headwaters of King-combe Inlet and Bella Coola River. He made the salmon ascend Bella Coola River up to Mount Smayā'na.

One winter Anoxema'axōts's brothers went out in their canoe to fish by the light of torches. Suddenly an avalanche came down Mount Nusq!e'lst, burying the village and killing Anoxema'axōts. One man who was living in this village had a post to which a copper was fastened. His house was not destroyed by the avalanche, and when the brothers returned they heard him shouting, and dug him out.

I obtained another curious tradition referring to Nana'tskuiɪ. Nana'tskuiɪ. lived at Na'us, which is near Kingcombe Inlet. His brothers were Q·ō'mo-qoya and Qoatsī'nas, the Raven. His sisters were Nūpɪɪxanē'ta and Pɪɪxanē'xas. They left their home and travelled for a long time, until they reached Sō'mxōɪ. on the lake above River's Inlet. There they found a small river. The Raven thought, " Why is this river so small, and the lake so large?" The Raven went up the river and discovered the cause. He found that the Beavers had dammed the whole river. He broke the beaver-dams, and the river increased very much in size. He saw the Beavers swimming by in the river, and he caught them. Then they went down the river. When they reached its mouth, Nana′tskuiᴸ took out a small house, which he put down. It increased in size at once, and became as large as a real house. He placed a post in front of the house, and put an eagle on top of it. They settled at this place.

The Raven, however, wished to travel all over the world. He spread his wings and departed. After some time he saw a copper. He alighted on top of it, and sat there with spread wings. His wings measured one fathom. The chief of this country was named Tai′taim ("copper"). He heard the noise of the Raven alighting. He arose and went out. He said to the Raven, "Why do you sit here? Come into my house. If you so desire, you may have this whole country for your own." The Raven entered the house. The interior of the house shone like fire. He was made to sit down in the rear of the house, and was treated well. They offered him all kinds of food, but he did not eat. Early in the morning, however, he ate copper plates. Tai′taim gave the Raven the sisau′k· dance, and gave him the names ᴸā′qoag·ila and Tai′taim.

Then the Raven returned. When he reached the house of his brother, he gave him two copper plates, asking him to use them as ornaments, and told him to use the Raven mask when dancing the sisau′k·. Following is his song : —

A - hai - yo - lai - ya   hē - ya - lai - ya   hai - yo - lai - ya   yā - la.
Ts′ᴇdēna yūdanaxuɩ ahaisōtaiya tsōnauēaxtēg·ina.
Aᴸ′aikᵘts nxˮauts qowisuᴸ′aix· siᴸ′aiā′utsutstki snōō′stxmîstsk·i.
Aᴇxmalōsuᴸ′a′x ta ᴸa′liasuᴸ′ax.

Then the Raven went up the river again. He saw a place which looked green and blue all over, and he desired very much to obtain possession of this beautiful color. When he came near, he saw that the ground was covered with abelone shells. He alighted. The chief of this country was called Pᴇlxanē′mx· ("abelone man"). He saw the Raven sitting on the shells, and invited him to come into his house; and he offered him the shells, saying that he might use them in his dance. Then he gave the Raven his hat. It was covered all over with abelone shells. He told him to wear his hat while dancing the sisau′k·, and gave him his name, Nōnukomō′tslaix·. Then he sent him back. When he reached his brother's house, he gave him a great many abelone shells.

Then he said to his sister, Pɛlxanē'xas, "Accompany me to Asē'ix" (on South Bentinck Arm). They started, and soon came to Ts'i'o, a lake a little above Asē'ix. He took along the eagle which was on the pole in front of his brother's house. Here they found the chief, At'ɛ'ntsit, who invited them to accompany him to his own river, calling the Raven his brother. But At'ɛ'ntsit coveted the Raven's abelone shells. Therefore the latter left him. He saw that the branches of the trees interlocked above the water of the river. He spread them apart. Then he went down the river. Near its mouth he saw smoke rising from a place. He was afraid to go there, thinking that the people might attack him; therefore he staid some distance from the village. He put up the pole surmounted by the eagle, and he took the name Nū'kunaʟaix·. Then he gave his sister the name Naayalx·aʟaix· ("making good trail"). He adorned both his houses with the abelone shells. A chief named Aʟk'untā'n. lived at Nokoā'koa'sta, on this river, opposite the place where the Raven had built his house.

One day the Crane alighted on top of the Raven's house, and was crying. The Raven thought, "What is crying on my house?" Then the Crane replied, "I am going to give you supernatural powers." The Crane, invited by the Raven, entered, and said, "Don't speak to me, just look at me." the evening the Crane went down to the river. He took the Raven's canoe and caught plenty of fish, so that the canoe was quite full. Then he returned to the house. The Eagle on top of the pole saw the canoe filled with salmon, and shouted for joy, "Tititititititi!" Then the people who lived on the opposite side of the river heard the Eagle, and asked each other, "Why does that Eagle cry early in the morning?" They crossed the river in their canoes; and when they found all the fish, they knew that the Raven was a successful fisherman. Every night the Crane went to catch fish. One evening he went down to the beach, and saw an object of very large size moving up towards the river. He thought, "I will harpoon it." He struck it, and when he hauled in his line, he saw that he had caught K·i'lx·ta (Plate XI, Fig. 8), the sea-monster whose skin is covered with pitch. All kinds of animals were glued to its skin. Then the Crane returned to the house, and gave the sea-monster to the Raven. It was to be his supernatural helper. Every time the Crane arrived, the Eagle cried, and all the people knew that he had caught an abundance of fish.

Another day the Crane went down to the sea again to catch fish, then he heard a noise as though some one were using a hammer, and he did not know what it was. The noise sounded nearer and nearer. Finally he saw a large canoe with many people, who were singing and beating time. The Crane thought, "I wish they would come near!" The canoe reached the point where he was sitting; then he cast his harpoon, and made fast the line. The people did not know what held them, and they made many efforts to free their canoe. But the Crane hauled in his line, and pulled the canoe ashore. Then the Crane said to the chief of the canoe, "I caught your canoe." The chief replied, "If you have succeeded in doing so, you have obtained me as your supernatural helper. This is the canoe 'Nō'ak·nɛm.' We carry food all over the world. What do you wish to have? Do you wish to have my box? You may have it. It is always full." But the Crane did not reply. He wished to have the chief's song. After a while the chief asked, "Do you wish to have my song?" Then the Crane replied in the affirmative, and the chief gave him the names K·a'ɪnspōxtamēm and Spu'xpuxtemēm.

The Crane returned to his house, and sang the song which he had obtained. The canoe returned to its own country. When the Crane approached the house, the Eagle cried with a different noise, because he knew that the Crane had obtained supernatural power. Then he entered, and said to the Raven, "I have found supernatural power, and captured a large canoe; and the chief of the canoe gave me his song and his dance, and he told me the name of the canoe. Take what I have found. The dance is called sqoa'lxoalɛm. When you perform this dance, use my mask. You shall never cease using this dance, and you shall give it to your children, and to your children's children."

V.

Before I begin to discuss these legends, I will give a number of traditions in detail, some of which illustrate the beliefs set forth in the preceding remarks, while others furnish important points of view for an investigation on the origin of the mythology of the tribe.

THE SALMON.[1]

In a place named K·ĭ'pōts, near Sɛnxl, on Bella Coola River, there used to be a salmon-weir. A chief lived at this place whose name was Sir ʊ'k!pt ("satiated") and Sĭ'ʟmak· ("salmon-weir"). His wife's name was Atsqutō'ʟ. One day she was cutting salmon on the bank of the river. When she opened the last salmon, she found a small boy in it. She took him out and washed him in the river. She placed him near by, entered the house, and said to the people, "Come and see what I have found in my salmon!" She had a child in her house, which was still in the cradle. The little boy whom she had found was half as long as her fore-arm. She

---

[1] Fillip Jacobsen records a version of this tradition in Ymer, 1894, pp. 193 ff. He calls the young man who visits heaven Kloma, which corresponds to ʟō'ma in my spelling.

carried him into the house, and the people advised her to take good care of him. She nursed him with her own baby. When the people were talking in the house, the baby looked around as though he understood what they were saying. On the following day the people were surprised to see how much he had grown, and in a few days he was as tall as an ordinary child. Her own baby also grew up with marvellous rapidity. She gave each of them one breast. After a few days they were able to walk and to talk.

The boys went to play on the bank of the river, and the Salmon boy said, "Let us make a little hut and play there. We will make two-pointed arrows and shoot birds." When the hut was completed, he sent the other boy back. He asked his friend to return at noon, and instructed him to shout when approaching the hut. He said, "You must always shout before you enter this hut. If you should ever forget to do so, I shall die. Then you must carry me to the water and place me on sticks. Then watch from a distance and see what will happen." Then he hid in the hut while his companion departed. At noon the latter returned in his canoe. When some distance from the hut he shouted. Soon he reached there, and found the hut full of birds, which the Salmon boy threw into the canoe, almost filling it. The boy returned to his father's house, and the people helped him unload the canoe. They built a large fire in the house, heated stones, and boiled water, in which they cooked the birds. On the following day the Salmon boy went again to his hut to shoot birds, but he did not catch any thing. The day after, he again asked his friend to come in his canoe to meet him. The hut was full of birds, and he filled the whole canoe. Thus he continued filling the boy's canoe with birds on alternate days. The people of the town were well provided with meat.

One day when the boy approached the hut in his canoe, he did not shout. He landed without making any noise, and went ashore. Suddenly he opened the door of the hut and said, "Let us go home." When he looked about, he saw a salmon lying on the floor almost dead, and quivering, and it was vomiting pieces of quartz. Then the boy was afraid. He returned to his mother, and said to her, "I forgot my brother's command, and opened the door too quickly, and found him dead." The people went to the hut, carried the salmon to the water, and placed it on sticks. The boy watched from a distance. He saw a canoe coming up the river, which was manned by many people. He thought, "It looks as though they were coming to see my brother." When the boat reached the place where the dead Salmon lay, one of the occupants of the canoe said, "We come to fetch you."—"Hm!" said the Salmon. He arose and went aboard. Then his brother shouted, "Wait for me! I will join you." The Salmon boy said to the steersman, "Keep near the bank of the river." The boy ran down to the bank and jumped aboard; then the canoe turned, going down the river. The other people in the canoe were unable to see him. They proceeded down the river, and finally arrived in the country of the Salmon. When they landed, they discovered the boy. One of them said, "Is not the Spring Salmon his mother?" The Salmon boy replied, "He is my brother."

The next day they proceeded on their journey, and the Salmon boy said to his brother, "Do not be afraid when we reach the shore of the next country, which is not far from here. There is a strong smell. Take a long breath before we reach it, and cover your nose with your hands." Then they reached the country of the Smelt. There was an overpowering stench off the coast; but he obeyed his brother's commands, took a long breath, covered his nose with his hands, and thus passed unharmed. Now the Salmon boy said, "Do not be afraid when we are passing the next place. Something will fall upon us like snow. Then shake yourself, that you may not be harmed." Soon they reached the place of the Herrings, and scales were falling in great numbers; but the boy shook himself, and the scales did not harm him. Now the Salmon boy said to his brother, "The next place that we shall reach is a very good one." When they reached the place, they found every thing covered with grease. It was the village of the Olachen. Then the Salmon boy said, "We are not very far from another village. It stands on a nice opening, and is a beautiful place to look at. You will see many children playing behind the houses." Soon they reached this place. Here they landed, and the Salmon boy ordered the other people to go on, while he himself staid there with his brother. It was the country of the Salmon. It was a large country. In the first house lived the Spring Salmon, in the second house the Sockeye Salmon, in the following the Hump-back Salmon. The Calico Salmon, the Dog Salmon, the Cohoes Salmon,—all lived there. Many canoes were on the bank of the river. Now they found the children who were playing behind the houses. One of the children said, "I smell something strange that does not belong to our country. It smells just like the country where we go every spring." They did not see the boy.

The two young men were passing by the houses, and looked into the doorways. There was a house in the centre of this town; there they saw a beautiful girl sitting in the middle of the house. Her hair was red, and reached down to the floor. She was very white. Her eyes were large, and as clear as rock crystal. The boy fell in love with the girl. They went on, but his thoughts were with her. The Salmon boy said, "I am going to enter this house. You must watch closely what I do, and imitate me. The Door of this house tries to bite every one who enters." The Door opened, and the Salmon jumped into the house. Then the Door snapped, but missed him. When it opened again, the boy jumped into the house. They found a number of people inside, who invited them to sit down. They spread food before them, but the boy did not like their food. It had a very strong smell, and looked rather curious. It consisted of algæ that grow on logs that lie in the river. When the boy did not touch it, one of the men said to him, "Maybe you want to eat those two children. Take them down to the river and throw them into the water, but do not look." The two children arose, and he took them down to the river. Then he threw them into the water without looking at them. At the place where he had thrown them down, he found a male and a female Salmon. He took them up to the house and roasted them. The people told him to preserve the intestines and the bones carefully. After he had eaten, one of the men told him to carry the intestines and the bones to the same place where he had thrown the children into the water. He carried them in his hands, and threw them into the river without looking. When he entered the house, he heard the children following him. The girl was covering one of her eyes with her hand. The boy was limping, because he had lost one of his bones. Then the people looked at the place where the boy had been sitting, and they found the eye, and a bone from the head of the male salmon. They ordered the boy to throw these into the water. He took the children and the eye and the bone, and threw them into the river. Then the children were hale and well.

After a while the youth said to his Salmon brother, "I wish to go to the other house where I saw the beautiful girl." They went there, and he said to his Salmon brother, "Let us enter. I should like to see her face well." They went in. Then the man arose, and spread a caribou blanket for them to sit on, and the people gave them food. Then he whispered to his brother, "Tell the girl I want to marry her." The Salmon boy told the girl, who smiled, and said, "He must not marry me. Whoever marries me must die. I like him, and I do not wish to kill him; but if he wishes to die, let him marry me. He may lie down by my side, but he must not cohabit with me. Tum ad litus iit, ubi lapides duos sustulit longos et rotundos. Cum advesperasset, lapidibus sub bracchio celatis cubiculum ingressus cum uxore decubuit. Salmonaceus puer autem cum eum ingredientem vidisset, eum prorsus perisse existimabat. Deinde adulescens ille cum uxore coire conabatur, sed eum his verbis repellebat: 'Num mori cupis? Fac finem orandi, nam tui me miseret.' Tum ille respondit: 'Num me mortalem tantum, unum e multis, esse putas? Immo illae orcae similis ego sum. Numquam igitur moriar.' Sic postquam adulescens impetravit ut mulier, precibus superata, eum secum coire pateretur, statim unum e lapidibus mulieris in vaginam inseruit. Vagina autem dentibus armata est qui lapidem momorderunt et molebant donec prope detritus est. Cum adulescens haec animadvertisset, lapide hoc exempto alterum in locum eius in vaginam condidit. Dentes iam prope consumpti erant quam ob rem lapidem huc illuc torquere incipiebat nec desiit dum prorsus eos sustulisset. Quod cum fecisset, hoc lapide item remoto penem iam inseruit. Hunc mulier arripuit sed nihil ei nocuit, dentes enim iam nulli fuerunt. Mox adulescentis amore flagrans mulier eum e lecto surgere non patiebatur. Item postridie mane cum ceteri mortales e lectis surrexissent, mulier ipsa e cubiculo exiit sed virum lecto haerere cogebat. Tum salmonaceus puer perterritus eam interrogavit: 'Occidistine fratrem meum? Coiitne tecum?' Respondit mulier: 'Sane mecum coiit nec mortuus est.' Puer autem ei credere nolebat, sed cum cubiculum ingressus esset fratrem vivum et incolumem vidit."

The woman was the Salmon-berry Bird. After one day she gave birth to a boy, and on the following day she gave birth to a girl. She was the daughter of the Spring Salmon.

After a while the girl's father said, "Let us launch our canoe, and let us carry the young man back to his own people." He sent a messenger to call all the people of the village; and they all made themselves ready, and early the next morning they started in their canoes. The young man went in the canoe of the Spring Salmon, which was the fastest. The canoe of the Sock-eye Salmon came next. The people in the canoe of the Calico Salmon were laughing all the time. They went up the river; and a short distance below the village of the young man's father they landed, and made fast their canoes. Then they sent two messengers up the river to see if the people had finished their salmon-weir. Soon they returned with information that the weir had been finished. Then they sent the young man and his wife, and they gave them a great many presents for the young man's father.

The watchman who was stationed at the salmon-weir saw two beautiful salmon entering the trap. They were actually the canoes of the salmon; but they looked to him like two salmon. Then the watchman put the traps down over the weir, and he saw a great many fish entering them. He raised the trap when it was full, and took the fish out. The young man thought, "I wish he would treat me and my wife carefully;" and his wish came true. The man broke the heads of the other salmon, but he saved the young man and his wife. Then he carried the fish up to the house, and hung them over a pole. During the night the young man and his wife resumed their human shape. The youth entered his father's house. His head was covered with eagle-down. He said to his father, "I am the fish whom you caught yesterday. Do you remember the time when you lost me? I have lived in the country of the Salmon. The Salmon accompanied me here. They are staying a little farther down the river. It pleases the Salmon to see the people eating fish." And, turning to his mother, he continued, "You must be careful when cutting Salmon. Never break any of their bones, but preserve them, and throw them into the water." The two children of the young man had also entered into the salmon-trap. He put some leaves on the ground, placed red and white cedar-bark over them, and covered them with eagle-down, and he told his mother to place the Salmon upon these.[1] As soon as he had given these instructions, the Salmon began to come up the river. They crossed the weir and entered the traps. They went up the river as far as Stū'ix·, and the people dried the Salmon according to his instructions. They threw the bones into the water, and the Salmon returned to life, and went back to their own country, leaving their meat behind. The Cohoes Salmon had the slowest canoe, and therefore he was the last to reach the villages. He gave many presents to the Indians. He gave them many-colored leaves, and thus caused the leaves of the trees to change color in the autumn.

Now all the Salmon had returned. The Salmon-berry Bird and her children had returned with them. Then the young man made up his mind to build a small hut, from which he intended to catch eagles. He used a long pole, to which a noose was attached. The eagles were baited by means of Salmon. He spread a mat in his little house, and when he had caught an eagle he pulled out its down. He accumulated a vast amount of down. Then he went back to his house and asked his younger brother to accompany him. When they came to the hut which he had used for catching eagles, he gave the boy a small staff. Then he said to him, " Do not be sorry when I leave you. I am going to visit the Sun. I am not going to stay away a long time. I staid long in the country of the Salmon, but I shall not stay long in heaven. I am going to lie down on this mat. Cover me with this down, and then begin to beat time with your staff. You will see a large feather flying upward, then stop." The boy obeyed, and every thing happened as he had said. The boy saw the feather flying in wide circles. When it reached a great height, it began to soar in large circles, and finally disappeared in the sky. Then the boy cried, and went back to his mother.

The young man who had ascended to heaven found there a large house. It was the House of Myths. There he resumed his human shape, and peeped in at the door. Inside he saw a number of people who were turning their faces toward the wall. They were sitting on a low platform in the rear of the house. In the right-hand corner of the house he saw a large fire, and women sitting around it. He leaned forward and looked into the

---

[1] This custom prevails up to this day. When the first salmon are caught, a stick wound with red cedar-bark is stuck into the ground at the bank of a river. (A specimen of this stick is in the Museum, Cat. No. $\frac{16}{1550}$.) A line is attached to it, and the salmon, after they have been caught, are strung on this line, which lies in the water. Then the Indians spread leaves of skunk cabbage on the ground, which are covered with a large coarse mat made of cedar-bark. On this mat red and white cedar-bark is placed as a pillow for the salmon. The people say " háqutó'i " (meaning unknown, said to be an archaic expression). Then they take small strips of cedar-bark and offer them to the salmon, saying, " Ēp'ax ōʟt'ai'x· qᴬmxamēlau· " (" Take this, salmon ;" qᴬmxamēlau· is an archaic name for the salmon). Next they strew eagle-down over the salmon, which is placed with its head on the cedar-bark. All the salmon that have been caught are laid side by side on the cedar-bark. Then they are carried up to the house and roasted.

house. An old woman discovered him, and beckoned him to come to her. He stepped up to her, and she warned him by signs not to go to the rear of the house. She said, "Be careful! The men in the rear of the house intend to harm you." She opened a small box, and gave him the bladder of a mountain-goat, which contained the cold wind. She told him to open the bladder if they should attempt to harm him. She said that if he opened it, no fire could burn him. She told him that the men were going to place him near the fire, in order to burn him; that one of them would wipe his face, then fire would come forth from the floor, scorching every thing. The old woman told him every thing that the people were going to do. Her name was SnŭLk'ulx·a'ls, or ALq'oalai'xElx·. Now the man in the rear of the house turned round. He was the Sun himself. He was going to try the strength of the visitor. When he saw the young man, he said to SnŭLk'ulx·a'ls, "Did anybody come to visit you? Let the young man come up to me. I wish him to sit down near me." The young man stepped up to the Sun, and as soon as he had sat down, the Sun wiped his face and looked at the young man (he had turned his face while he was wiping it). Then the young man felt very hot. He tied his blanket tightly round his body, and opened the bladder which the woman had given him. Then the cold wind that blows down the mountains in the winter was liberated, and he felt cool and comfortable. The Sun had not been able to do him any harm. The old man did not say any thing, but looked at his visitor.

After a while he said, "I wish to show you a little underground house that stands behind this house." They both rose and went outside. The small house had no door. Access was had to it by an opening in the centre of the roof, through which a ladder led down to the floor. Not a breath of air entered this house. It was made of stone. When they had entered, the Sun made a small fire in the middle of the house; then he climbed up the ladder and closed the door, leaving his visitor inside. The Sun pulled up the ladder, in order to make escape impossible. Then the house began to grow very hot. When the boy felt that he could not stand the heat any longer, he opened the bladder, and the cold wind came out; snow began to fall on the fire, which was extinguished; icicles began to form on the roof, and it was cool and comfortable inside. After a while the Sun said to his four daughters, "Go to the little underground house that stands behind our house, and sweep it," meaning that they were to remove the remains of the young man whom he believed to be burned. They obeyed at once, each being eager to be the first to enter. When they opened the house, they were much surprised to find icicles hanging down from the roof.

They climbed down the ladder, and the youth, looking up, saw their genitalia. When they were coming down, he arose and scratched them.

The youngest girl was the last to step down. The girls cried when the youth touched them, and ran away. The Sun heard their screams, and asked the reason. He was much surprised and annoyed to hear that the young man was still alive. Then he devised another way of killing his visitor. He told his daughters to call him into his house. They went, and the young man re-entered the House of Myths. In the evening he lay down to sleep. Then the Sun said to his daughters, " Early to-morrow morning climb the mountain behind our house. I shall tell the boy to follow you." The girls started while the visitor was still asleep. The girls climbed up to a   all meadow which was near a precipice. They had taken the form of mountain-goats. When the Sun saw his daughters on the meadow, he called to his visitor, saying, " See those mountain-goats !" The young man arose when he saw the mountain-goats. He wished to kill them. The Sun advised him to walk up the right-hand side of the mountain, saying that the left-hand side was dangerous. The young man carried his bow and arrow. The Sun said, " Do not use your own arrows ! Mine are much better." Then they exchanged arrows, the Sun giving him four arrows of his own. The points of these arrows were made of coal. Now the young man began to climb the mountain. When he came up to the goats, he took one of the arrows, aimed it, and shot. It struck the animal, but fell down without killing it. The same happened with the other arrows. When he had spent all his arrows, they rushed up to him from the four sides, intending to kill him. His only way of escape was in the direction of the precipice. They rushed up to him, and pushed him down the steep mountain. He fell headlong, but when he was halfway down he transformed himself into a ball of bird's down. He alighted gently on a place covered with many stones. There he resumed the shape of a man, arose, and ran into the house of the Sun to get his own arrows. He took them, climbed the mountain again, and found the mountain-goats on the same meadow. He shot them and killed them, and threw them down t' e precipice ; then he returned. He found the goats at the foot of the precipice, and cut off their feet. He took them home. He found the Sun sitting in front of the house. He offered him the feet, saying, " Count them, and see how many I have killed." The Sun counted them, and now he knew that all his children were dead. Then he cried, " You killed my children !" Then the youth took the bodies of the goats, fitted the feet on, and threw the bodies into a little river that was running past the place where they had fallen down. Thus they were restored to life. He had learned this art in the country of the Salmon. Then he said to the girls, " Now run to see your father ! He is wailing for you." They gave him a new name, saying, " Sᴌ'ᴇ'mstalalôst'aix' has restored us to life." The boy followed them. Then the Sun said, when he entered, " You shall marry my two eldest daughters."

On the next morning the people arose. Then the Sun said to them, "What shall I do to my son-in-law?" He called him, and said, "Let us raise the trap of my salmon-weir." They went up to the river in the Sun's canoe. The water of the river was boiling. The youth was in the bow of the canoe, while the Sun was steering. He caused the canoe to rock, intending to throw the young man into the water. The water formed a small cascade, running down over the weir. He told the young man to walk over the top of the weir in order to reach the trap. He did so, walking over the top beam of the weir. When he reached the baskets, the beam fell over, and he himself fell into the water. The Sun saw him rise twice in the whirlpool just below the weir. When he did not see him rise again, he turned his canoe, and thought, "Now the boy has certainly gone to Nusk·ya'xêk·." The Sun returned to his house, and said to his daughters, "I lost my son-in-law in the river. I was not able to find him." Then his daughters were very sad.

When the boy disappeared in the water, he was carried to Nusk·ya'xêk·; and he resumed the shape of a salmon while in the water, and as soon as he landed he resumed human shape and returned to his wife. The Sun saw him coming, and was much surprised. In the evening they went to sleep. On the following morning the Sun thought, "How can I kill my son-in-law?" After a while he said to him, "Arise! We will go and split wood for fuel." He took his tools. They launched their canoe, and went down the river to the sea. When they reached there, it was perfectly calm. There were many snags embedded in the mud in the mouth of the river, some of which were only half submerged. They selected one of these snags a long distance from the shore, and began to split it. Then the Sun intentionally dropped his hammer into the water, and thought at the same time, "Do not fall straight down, but fall sideways, so that he will have much difficulty in finding you." Then he sat down in his canoe, and said, "Oh! I lost my old hammer. I had it at the time when the Sun was created." He looked down into the water, and did not say a word. After a while he said to the young man, "Do you know how to dive? Can you get my hammer? The water is not very deep here." The young man did not reply. Then the Sun continued, "I will not go back without my hammer." Then the boy said, "I know how to dive. If you so wish, I will try to get it." The Sun promised to give him supernatural power if he was able to bring the hammer back. The youth jumped into the water, and then the Sun ordered the sea to rise, and he called the cold wind to make the water freeze. It grew so cold that a sheet of ice a fathom thick was formed at once on top of the sea. "Now," he thought, "I certainly have killed you!" He left his canoe frozen up in the ice, and went home. He said to his daughters, "I have lost my son-in-law. He drifted away when the cold winds began to blow down the mountains. I have also lost my little hammer." But when he mentioned his hammer, his daughters knew at once what had happened. The young man found the hammer, and after he had obtained it he was going to return to the canoe, but he struck his head against the ice, and was unable to get out. He tried everywhere to find a crack. Finally he found a very narrow one. He transformed himself into a fish, and came out of the crack. He jumped about on the ice in the form of a fish, and finally resumed his own shape. He went back to the Sun's house, carrying the hammer. The Sun was sitting in front of the fire, his knees drawn up, and his legs apart. His eyes were closed, and he was warming himself. The young man took his hammer and threw it right against his stomach, saying, "Now take better care of your treasures." The young man scolded the Sun, saying, "Now stop trying to kill me. If you try again, I shall kill you. Do you think I am an ordinary man? You cannot conquer me." The Sun did not reply. In the evening he said to his son-in-law, "I hear a bird singing, which I should like very much to have." The young man asked, "What bird is it?" The Sun replied, "I do not know it. Watch it early to-morrow morning." The young man resolved to catch the bird. Very early in the morning he arose, then he heard the bird singing outside :—

(tremolo)

He knew at once that it was the sku'latᴇn ("ptarmigan"?). He left the house, and thought, "I wish you would come down!" Then the bird came down, and when it was quite near by he shot it. He hit one of its wings, intending to catch it alive. He waited for the Sun to arise. The bird understood what the young man said, who thus spoke: "The chief here wishes to see you. Do not be afraid, I am not going to kill you. The chief has often tried to kill me, but he has been unable to do so. You do not need to be afraid." The young man continued, "When it is dark I shall tell the Sun to ask you to sit near him, and when he is asleep I want you to peck out his eyes." When the Sun arose, the youth went into the house carrying the bird, saying, "I have caught the bird; now I hope you will treat it kindly. It will awaken us when it is time to arise. When you lie down, let it sit down near you, then it will call you in the morning." In the evening the Sun asked the bird to sit down next to his face. When he was asleep, the bird pecked out his eyes without his knowing it. Early in the morning he heard the bird singing. He was going to open his eyes, but he was not able to do so. Then he called his son, saying, "The bird has blinded me." The young man jumped up and went to his father-in-law, and said, "Why did you wish for the bird? Do you think it is good? It is a bad bird. It has pecked out your eyes." He took the bird and carried it outside, and thanked it for having done as it was bidden. Then the bird flew away. When it was time for the Sun to start on his daily course, he said, "I am afraid I might fall, because I cannot see my way." For four days he staid in his house. He did not eat, he was very sad. Then his son-in-law made up his mind to cure him. He did not do so before, because he wanted to punish him for his badness. He took some water, and said to his father-in-law, "I will try to restore your eyesight." He threw the water upon his eyes, and at once his eyes were healed and well. He said, "Now you can see what power I have. The water with which I have washed my face has the power to heal diseases. While I was in the country of the Salmon, I bathed in the water in which the old Salmon bathed, in order to regain youth, therefore the water in which I wash makes every thing young and well." From this time on, the Sun did not try to do any harm to the young man.

Finally he wished to return to his father's village. He left the house, and jumped down through the hole in heaven. His wife saw him being transformed into a ball of eagle-down, which floated down gently. Then her father told her to climb as quickly as she could down his eyelashes. She did so, and reached the ground at the same time as her husband. He met his younger brother, who did not recognize him. He had been in heaven for one year.

THE SNENE'IQ.

Once upon a time there was a youth whose name was Anutxo'ôts, who was playing with a number of girls behind the village. While they were playing, a noise like the cracking of twigs was heard in the woods. The noise came nearer and nearer. The youth hid behind a tree, and saw that a Snēnē'iq was approaching. She was chewing gum, which caused the noise. He advised the children to run away, but they did not obey. When they saw the gum, they stepped up to the Snēnē'iq and asked her to give them some. The Snēnē'iq gave a piece of gum to all the children, and when she saw Anutxo'ôts, who was advising the children to return home, she took him and threw him into the basket which she was carrying on her back. Then she took all the other children and threw them on top of him into her basket. After she had done so, she turned homeward. Then Anutxo'ôts whispered to the girls to take off their cedar-bark blankets, and to escape through a hole that he was going to cut in the basket. He took his knife, cut a hole in the bottom of the basket, and fell down. The girls also fell down one by one until only one of them was left.

All the children returned home and told their parents what had happened. The mother of the girl who had not been able to escape began to cry, mourning for her daughter. She cried for four days and four nights. Then her nose began to swell, because she had been rubbing it all the time. She had thrown the mucus of her nose on the ground. Now when she looked down, she saw that something was moving at the place where it had fallen. She watched it from the corners of her eyes, and soon she discovered that her mucus was assuming the shape of a little child. The next time she looked, the child had grown to the size of a new-born baby. Then the woman took it up, and the child began to cry. She carried it into the house, and washed the baby for four days. Then the child, who was very pretty and had red hair, began to speak, and said, "My father, the Sun, sent me to ask you to stop crying. I shall go out into the woods, but pray don't cry, for I am sent to recover your daughter. I know where she is. Make a small salmon-spear for me, which I shall need." Thus spoke the boy.

Then the woman asked an old man to make a salmon-spear, which she gave to her son. His mother gave him ear-rings made of abelone shells, and the boy played about with his spear, and always wore his ear ornaments. One day when his mother was crying again, the boy said, "Mother, I ask you once more, don't cry, for my father the Sun sent me down to bring back your daughter. He will show me where she is. I shall start to-day to recover my sister from the Snēnē'iq, who stole her. Don't worry about me." Then the boy went up the river Qoā'ᴌna. After he had gone some distance, he came to a tree which overhung the river. He climbed it, and looked down in order to see if there were any fish in the water. Soon he heard a noise some distance up the stream, and gradually it sounded nearer. Then he saw the Snēnē'iq coming down the river. When she reached the tree, she stopped and looked down into the clear water. She saw the image of the boy, who was sitting on the tree, and thought it was her own reflection. She said, "How pretty I am!" and she brushed her hair back out of her face. When she did so, the boy imitated her movements in order to make her believe that she was looking at her own reflection. When she laughed, he laughed also, in order to deceive her. But at last the Snēnē'iq looked upward, and saw the boy sitting in the tree. Then she addressed him with kindly words, and asked him to come down. She said, "What did your mother do in order to make you so pretty?" The boy replied, "You cannot endure the treatment I had to undergo in order to become as pretty as I am." The Snēnē'iq begged, "Oh, come down and tell me. I am willing to stand even the greatest pain in order to become as pretty as you are. What are you doing up there?" Then the boy said, "I was watching for salmon, which I desire to harpoon with my salmon-spear." The Snēnē'iq repeated, "Oh, come down, and do with me whatever you please in order to make me as pretty as you are." The boy replied, "I don't believe you can endure the wounds that I have to inflict upon you." She replied, "You may cut me as much as you please. I want to become as pretty as you are." Then the boy climbed down the tree, and the Snēnē'iq asked, "What must we do first?" He said, "We must go up this river Anuᴌxu'mxmē to find two stone knives with which my mother used to cut off my head." They walked up the river, and found the stone knives. Then the boy said to the Snēnē'iq, "Now lie down on this stone. Put your neck on this knife." The Snēnē'iq did as she was bidden. Then the boy took the other knife, told the Snēnē'iq to shut her eyes, and cut off her head. The head jumped back to the body, and was about to unite with it, when the boy passed his hands over the wound, and thus prevented the severed head from joining the body again. Thus he had killed her.

Then he went to the Snēnē'iq's house. He found his sister whom the Snēnē'iq had killed and smoked over her fire. He took the body down, and patted it all over with his hands. Thus he resuscitated the girl. On looking around in the house, he found the dried bodies of other children, whom he also brought back to life. Then he took the girl and the other children home.

Now the boy was grown up. His mother was very glad. She wanted him to marry. She selected a girl to be his wife. They built a house. He ordered his wife to sleep in the bedroom on the right in the rear corner of the house, while he himself slept in the left-hand rear corner. After four days his wife had a son, who grew up very fast. One day the young man said to his mother, "Do you know my name? Do you know whose son I am?" His mother replied that she did not know. Then he said, "My name is 'Son of the Sun.' It is now time for me to return to my father. Don't allow any one to harm my son, for I shall guard him; and don't feel sorry about me when I disappear. Now go and gather some eagle-down." His mother went from house to house, begging the people to give her some eagle-down. The people brought it to her house. Once more he charged his mother to guard his son well, and he threatened to take revenge upon any person who should harm him. He continued, "Don't mourn about me, for to-morrow I shall go home to my father, who sent me to recover your daughter. He heard you crying, and wanted me to come to your assistance." His mother replied, "I shall try not to mourn for you, but you know that I have loved you ever since you were born. I love you now on account of your works." Then the son of the Sun continued, "My son shall take my name."

On the following morning he carried the eagle-down out of the house. He placed it on the ground, and all the people assembled to see what would happen. He told his boy to beat time on a board, and at once the eagle-down began to ascend to the sky like smoke. He jumped into the down and was wafted upward. The people noticed a strong wind blowing upward, and the young man had disappeared.

THE SNĒNĒ'IQ.[1]

Once upon a time the people of Q'ō'mqūtis found that the bodies from their burial-ground were being carried away. They accused one another of robbing the graves. In one of their disputes a man by the name of Kxua'naᴛ arose and said, "I do not think that any human being is robbing our grave-yards. Our ancestors told us that the Snēnē'iq (Plate VII, Fig. 7) carries away the bodies. I will pretend to be dead, and you shall bury me. Then I shall discover who is carrying away the bodies." His sister begged him not to do so, but he persisted. Then the tribe agreed to it. They placed him in a box, and carried him to the graveyard. Then his sister and all the women began to wail, as is customary, "Ananai' qamatsai'!" ("Ananai', my dear!") In the evening one of Kxua'naᴛ's friends hid near the grave. After a while he saw a large black being approaching the grave. It was the Snēnē'iq, who broke the box, took out the man, threw him into the basket that he carried on his shoulders, and started to go up the river. Then Kxua'naᴛ's friend shouted, "Hold on to the branches of the trees! We will try to rescue you." Then he ran back to the village and aroused the people. They took up their torches, and started in search of the tracks of the Snēnē'iq.

Kxua'naᴛ watched his opportunity, and when he saw the branch of a tree overhanging the trail, he held on to it; but the Snēnē'iq pulled with all his strength, thus compelling Kxua'naᴛ to let go his hold. Then the Snēnē'iq fell down forward, his basket tumbled over his head, and the man dropped to the ground. Then the Snēnē'iq broke wind and the man began to smile. The Snēnē'iq observed that he was moving, and said, "Is this a dead salmon?" (qamxamilau' nuquawaxa'; he called the man a salmon.) The Snēnē'iq put his hand on the man's chest, in order to feel if the latter were breathing. Then Kxua'naᴛ kept perfectly quiet, and as soon as the Snēnē'iq felt re-assured that the man was dead, he threw him into his basket and went off again.

When the day dawned, the Snēnē'iq arrived at his house. There he placed the man on the floor. Kxua'naᴛ blinked with his eyes, and saw the old Snēnē'iq, his wife, and his two young ones, sitting round the fire. On the left-hand side of the door there was a harpoon. He resolved to try to take this harpoon if he should succeed in making his escape. Then the

[1] I published another version of this legend in Verhandlungen der Berliner Gesellschaft für Anthropologie Ethnologie und Urgeschichte, 1894, pp. 290, 291.

young Snēnē'iqs stepped up to the man, took hold of his testicles, and said, "These will be our ear ornaments." But the old Snēnē'iq remarked, "Don't say that. I am not sure if this is the right kind of salmon. I never caught anything like it. It was so heavy that I was hardly able to reach our house." He sharpened his knife, spread a mat on the floor close to the man, and placed the latter on it. Then he blew on the man's chest, as the Indians do when they begin to cut a bear. As soon as he began to cut, the blood flowed. Kxua'naL jumped up, clapped his hands together, and the four Snēnē'iqs were so much frightened that they all fainted. Kxua'naL took the harpoon and ran out of the house down the mountain. When he had almost reached Bilqula River, he heard the Snēnē'iq, who was pursuing him. The monster was about to overtake him. Then the man jumped into the river, for the Snēnē'iq is unable to swim. Finally Kxua'naL went ashore again, and reached his own village.

He invited the people to his house, told them of his adventure, and proposed to them to kill the Snēnē'iq. He told the people to gather together all the cast-off cedar-bark towels and cedar-bark blankets that lay under their houses, and to take a large bucket full of urine. They did so, took their bows and arrows, and went up the river until they came to NuLLē'ix. The Snēnē'iq's house was on top of a mountain near by. They climbed the mountain, and when they approached the house they saw the Snēnē'iq sitting in front of his house. When he looked at them, lightning came out of his eyes and made the people faint. Nevertheless they continued to climb the mountain. They attacked the Snēnē'iq with their bows and arrows, and he retired into his house, shutting the door behind him. Then they tied the cedar-bark blankets and towels, which they had brought along, to the ends of long poles, ignited them, and pushed the burning cedar-bark into the Snēnē'iq's house. They poured the urine into the house. The poisonous smoke of the old cedar-bark and of the urine made the Snēnē'iq, his wife, and his children sick. They began to cough and to sneeze, but very soon every thing was quiet. Then Kxua'naL and his friends opened the door and took off the roof boards, and they found that all the Snēnē'iqs were dead. The people went into the house, and took all the wealth that was there accumulated. Then they returned home.

THE SNĒNĒ'IQ.[1]

In early times the people in NuLLē'ix lived in underground lodges, the entrance to which was through a hole in the middle of the roof. One night a woman was awakened by a noise on the roof of the house. On looking

---

[1] I published another version of this legend in Verhandlungen der Berliner Gesellschaft für Anthropologie, Ethnologie und Urgeschichte, 1894, p. 288.

up, she saw something looking down the entrance. Then she aroused her husband. He thought that an enemy was about to attack them. He did not arise, but took his bow and arrow, which lay near by, and shot. He hit the throat of the supposed enemy, and heard him rolling down the roof of the house. As soon as it grew daylight he went out, but he did not find any thing.

On the next day one of the people of the village went up the river. He heard loud wailing some distance up the river. The cries were so loud that they frightened him, and he returned. He reported to his friends what he had heard, and a great many men went up the river, but they were all frightened by the noise. Finally a young man by the name of Koānatoℓai'x· offered to go and see what was causing the noise. He went up the river in his canoe, accompanied by one friend, and they saw a large Snēnē'iq sitting on a flat rock. As soon as the young man saw her, he began to imitate her wails. Then the Snēnē'iq said, "Come here! I am glad that you join in my wails, for I lost my son. I will return your kindness. My son, whom I lost, had a house on this mountain. You may go and take every thing that you see there." Then the Snēnē'iq arose, took a copper on which she was sitting, and presented it to the young man; and she told him that in her son's house he would find a variety of masks, which he should use in the kū'siut. She said, "I am going to leave this country now, and shall go to Na'us." The young man returned, and showed the copper to his father. He invited the people to accompany him to the Snēnē'iq's house. They started, and arrived at the place where the Snēnē'iq had been sitting. There they searched for the trail up the mountain. After looking for some time, they found the body of the young Snēnē'iq, the arrow still sticking in his throat. He had died while trying to return to his house. Thus they discovered the trail. They covered the body with bushes, and climbed up the mountain. When Koānatoℓai'x· entered the house, he found great quantities of meat, tallow, great numbers of skins, and many masks. He carried these home, and distributed the meat and the skins. In winter, when dancing the kū'siut, he used the masks which he had found.

THE SNĒNĒ'IQ.[1]

Once upon a time there was a girl who asked her mother for some mountain-goat tallow. Her mother did not give her any, and she began to cry. Finally the girl said, "If you do not give me any tallow, I shall cry all night." Then the mother took up a pair of tongs and struck the girl, saying, "If you do not stop crying, I shall turn you out of the house, and

---

[1] I published another version of this legend in Verhandlungen der Berliner Gesellschaft für Anthropologie, Ethnologie und Urgeschichte, 1894, pp. 288 ff.

the Snēnē'iq will come and take you away." Then the girl cried, "I wish the Snēnē'iq would come and take me." All of a sudden they heard some one trying to open the door, and saying, "Come here, I will give you some tallow." The girl said, "Now I shall get what I desire;" but her mother warned her, saying, "Don't go. I think that is the Snēnē'iq. I will give you some tallow now." But the girl refused to obey. She ran to the house door and opened it. The Snēnē'iq took her, threw her into her basket, and carried her to her house. She spoke very kindly to her, and offered to fetch her little sister as a playmate; but the girl asked her for the tallow which she had promised. While the Snēnē'iq was gone to get the tallow, the girl felt somebody touching her rabbit-skin blanket. She looked around, and saw an old woman sitting just behind her on the floor of the house. The old woman said, "Don't eat the tallow that she has gone to fetch. It is not mountain-goat tallow, but it is the fat of dead people. Also don't touch any of the berries that she may bring you, for they are insects, and if you eat them a root will grow from your back, and you will not be able to move. I ate from her food, and a root grew from my back into the ground, so that I cannot move. If she offers to bring your little sister, ask her to do so, and then I will show you how you may kill her. There is only one box in which she keeps food that you may eat. It stands in that corner. Ask her to give you food from that box."

After a while the Snēnē'iq came with a small basket of berries. She said to the girl, I have been picking berries for you. Now eat. They are good and sweet." But the girl refused, saying, "Those are not berries, those are insects, and I don't eat them." Then she threw the basket into the fire; and as soon as what seemed to be berries touched the fire, they began to run in all directions. Next the Snēnē'iq went to fetch some tallow. When she brought it to the girl, the latter said, "I don't eat man's fat, I want to have mountain-goat tallow." Then the Snēnē'iq was surprised. She said, "I will go now and fetch your sister." The girl encouraged her, saying that she felt lonely.

In the evening the Snēnē'iq started to fetch the girl. Then the old woman addressed the girl, saying, "Now you must kill the Snēnē'iq. If you don't do so, you will never return to your home. I was carried away by her. I ate of her food, and now a root holds me to the ground; and if any one tries to cut it, I must die. If you stay here more than four nights, a root will grow from your back, and fasten you to the floor of the house. It is easy to kill her." The girl replied, "She is so large, and I am so small, how shall I accomplish such a feat?" Then the old woman continued, "Do you see the mountain-goat horns in that corner of the house? Take ten of those, and put one on each finger, and one on each thumb. When the Snēnē'iq comes back to-morrow morning, stand at the door of this house, so that she will see you, put the mountain-goat horns on so that they cannot fall off, and then open and close your hands and sing, 'Yi, yi, yi! Open your eyes, close your eyes, and fall down, open your eyes, close your eyes, and fall down!' Watch to-night, that she may not surprise us."

On the following morning, as soon as the Snēnē'iq came in sight, the girl put the horns on her fingers and thumbs, and stood in the doorway; but the old woman instructed her to wait until the Snēnē'iq had climbed halfway up the steep mountain-side. Then the girl began to sing, and opened and closed her hands to the rhythm of the tune. Then the Snēnē'iq cried, "Please don't do that. If I fall down, you will never be able to come down the mountain." But the girl kept on singing until the Snēnē'iq fell backward, and rolled down the mountain. Then she entered the house and told the old woman that the Snēnē'iq was dead. The old woman instructed her to climb down the mountain, and to look for the body of the Snēnē'iq, and burn it, and to blow the ashes to the four winds. She obeyed, and the ashes were transformed into mosquitoes. Then the girl returned to the house.

Now the old woman asked her to bring some cedar-bark. When she had received it, she made four baskets. She told the girl to put meat, tallow, and blankets into these baskets. The meat and the blankets which she put in became exceedingly small, so that she was able to place vast amounts in the baskets. Then the woman instructed her to enter the secret room in the left-hand corner of the house. There the girl found red cedar-bark for all the various dances, and a great number of masks. She put these into one of the baskets. Then the old woman sent her home. She went, carrying the baskets.

When she came to the rear of her father's house, she put down the four baskets, and went to the street. There she was found, and led into the house. She told her father to send a man to fetch the four small baskets which she had left behind the house. He sent four strong men, but they were unable to lift the baskets. Then she went out herself, and returned, carrying all of them. As soon as she placed them on the floor of the house, the baskets grew to an enormous size. She took out the meat, the tallow, and the blankets, and her father distributed them among the people. In the winter dance she used the masks and the cedar-bark that she had obtained.

THE RAVEN.

There was a widow with a beautiful daughter. The Raven married the widow, but soon began to covet the daughter, and to think how he could get possession of her. Now he had devised a plan. He did not light a fire in his house for two days, until the girl began to complain of the cold. Then he offered to go to get firewood. First he went to the alder, made a cut in its bark, and asked, "What do you do when you are thrown into the fire?" The Alder replied, "I burn very quietly and steadily." Then the Raven retorted, "You are not the one whom I want." Next he went to the pine, made a cut in its bark, and asked, "What do you do when you are thrown into the fire?" The Pine retorted, "My nose runs and the fire crackles." "You are not the one whom I want," said the Raven. He went to the red cedar, made a cut in its bark, and asked, "What do you do when you are thrown into the fire?" Tum Thuya respondit, "In gremium mulierum insilio quae forte prope ignem sedent." "Forsitan," inquit corvus, "te velim. Nisi quem meliorem invenero, revertar." Cum ad Pseudotsugam mucronatam venisset, ex cortice eius quaesivit, "Quid tu facis, cum in ignem inieceris?" "Si me erectum ponis," respondit cortex, "recta puellarum in gremium incido quae prope ignem sunt." "Te demum," inquit corvus, "cupio." Cum corticis frusta adscidisset et ea orasset ut se adiuvaret in puella potienda, ea domum tulit et in focum imposuit. Cum ignis conflatus esset, puellam haud procul sedere iussit ut se fovere posset. "Primum tergus," inquit, "postea pectus in ignem converte. Deinde conside et pedes extende ut commode refovearis." Dum sic sedet, in gremium eius cortex, ut promiserat, incidit ut genitalia ureret. Puellae lamentanti corvus, "Remedium optimum," inquit, "cognovi, quod tibi statim medebitur. Herba autem in silvis est cuius erecta stirps semper sursum deorsum movetur. Hanc tu quaere et cum inveneris ei inside." Cum puella eius dicto oboediens exisset, corvus ipse domo egressus se in silvas abdidit et arena se ita texit ut penis tantum emineret. His comparatis optabat ut puella ad se veniret, quod cum fecisset, quasi quendam stirpitem sursum deorsum se moventem vidit, sed cum diligentius inspexisset et corvi oculos agnovisset, eo vehementer verberato domum rediit. Sic corvus misellus graviter spe deiectus est.

Then he planned what to do next. At this time Mŏ'xmuk''t (a bird living on the mountains) invited all the people to a feast. The Raven was not invited, and he planned how to obtain the food that they were preparing. He pretended to be sick, and said to his two children, "It is ridiculous that Mŏ'xmuk''t pretends to be a chief. He has nothing but leaves to eat. But you had better go and see what kind of food he is preparing." Then the two young Ravens went, and saw that he was broiling meat. When the food was almost done, the Raven arose, and crept stealthily behind the house at which all the guests were assembled. By this time the meat was done, and the people were placing it on long planks. Then he cried, "Wīna, wīna, wīna, wīna'! ēx·a, ēx·a, ēx·a, ēx·a'!" Then the people stopped, and said, "Who is crying there?" But the Raven ran home as quickly as possible, and lay down by the side of the fireplace. He asked his children to strew ashes over his body so as to avert suspicion of his having left the house.

Now the people sent two messengers to the Raven's house, in order to see if he might have uttered the cries; but they saw him lying down near the fireplace, and noticed that he was covered with ashes. Then the messengers returned, and reported what they had seen. The people discussed the meaning of the cries, and finally resolved to send to the Raven, who was renowned on account of his experience, and to ask his opinion. Two messengers went to see him. When they asked him, he said, "Those cries mean that your enemies will come to kill you. Escape while there is yet time. Don't stop to take your food along, but run away." The people followed his advice. He said, "I cannot join you, because I am sick. It does not matter whether the enemies kill me or whether I die of disease." As soon as the people had left, he arose, took all the meat, and hid it near his own house. On the following morning the people returned, and saw that the village was undisturbed, only the meat had disappeared. They looked askance at the Raven, suspecting that he had stolen their meat.

On the following day the Raven thought, "I will go to visit the Deer." He went there, opened the door of the Deer's house, and said, "At what season are you fattest?" The Deer replied, "At the time when the people have dried all their fish." Then the Raven left him, and returned at the time when all the fish had been dried. He said, "Lēqumai', come! I want to speak to you. Let us go up the mountain, and let us tell about our ancestors." They went up the mountain; and the Raven said, "Here is the place where I am accustomed to sit and to bask in the sun. Let us sit down here." It was a meadow near a steep precipice. The Raven induced the Deer to sit down near the precipice, while he himself sat down a little farther back. Now he supported his head on his hand, and began to cry, "How long your forelegs are, how long your forelegs are!" Then the Deer looked at him. The Raven said, "Now you must cry next." Then the Deer began to cry, and sang, "How gray your nose is!" And the Raven retorted, singing, "How long your nose is!"

Thus they continued for some time. When they had finished crying, the Raven asked, "How long have you been in this world?" The Deer replied, "It is a long time that I have been here. Tell me first how long you have been here." Then the Raven said, "I became a man when the mountains began to rise." The Deer retorted, "That is not so long. I am older than you are. I became a man before the Sun gave the world its present form." Then they began to cry again; and this time the Deer sang, "How ugly his foot is! His foot is all covered with scars." Then the Raven grew angry, pushed the Deer, and threw him down the precipice. Then he assumed the shape of the Raven, and flew down the mountain, crying, "Qoax!" He ate part of the Deer's meat, and concealed the rest under stones.

Then he returned home and lay down. He thought, "What shall I do next?" He made up his mind to travel. After some time he reached a house the door of which was open. He stepped in and looked about. He saw that the house was full of dried fish, which was moving as though women were working at it; but he did not see anybody. Then he went out and called his sisters Stsuwaastɛ'lqs ("crow"), Nuk·'ĕxnɛ'm ("mouse"), X·ilx· ("gull"), and K·'ĕxwa'qs ("rat"). He told them what he had seen, and asked them to help him carry away the provisions. He said, "I do not see any people; but implements moving by themselves are at work on the provisions." They entered the house, and the Raven took the fish down from the drying-frames, and asked his sisters to pack it into baskets and to carry it away. After he had thrown all the fish down, he descended to the floor of the house, and intended to go out; but he felt himself held by arms and feet, and was beaten without mercy. His sisters were treated in the same manner. They were taken, and their private parts rubbed over his face. Then he found that the Echo inhabited this house.

He returned home, and thought what to do next. He was hungry, and was glad when, after a little while, Maxuat!ā'laqa (a small water-fowl) invited him to his house. He accepted the invitation, and sat down near the fire. Then Maxuat!ā'laqa took a box, held his foot over it, and cut his ankle with a stone knife. At once salmon-eggs fell down into the box, filling it entirely. The Raven ate, and carried home to his sisters what was left over.

On the next morning a woman named K'uĕla'is ("young seal") invited him to a feast. He sat down near the fire, and she took a dish. She cleaned it, placed it near the fire, and held her hands over it. Then grease dropped down into the dish, filling it entirely. She gave it to the Raven, who ate heartily, and took home to his sisters what was left over.

On the following day the bird Aix·'a'xonē invited him to a feast. He placed a box near the fire and sang.

Aix· - a - xo-nē xo-nē xo-nē   qāx.

At once the box was full of salmon-berries. The Raven ate, and carried home to his sisters what was left over.

Now he resolved to invite Maxuat!ā'laqa. On the following day the bird came. Then the Raven took a box, put his foot into it, and cut his ankle, but nothing came out of it; and he said to Maxuat!ā'laqa, "Go back! I have nothing to give to you." In the evening he made up his mind to invite the young Seal. He felt of his hands all the time, to see if fat were dripping from them. On the next morning he invited her. He placed a mat for her near the fire, took a dish, cleaned it, and placed it on the mat. Then he held his hands over the dish, but not a particle of fat dripped out of them. His hands, however, were burnt to a crisp by the heat of the fire. Then he said to the Seal, "Go back! I have no food for you." Then he invited the bird Aix·'a'xonē. He placed a box near the fire, and tried to sing the bird's song; but there was only a single berry in the box. He continued, but did not succeed any better. Finally he sang "mEnk·," and the box was full of excrements.

On the following day he made up his mind to marry the sockeye Salmon. He said to his sisters, "Let us go to the Salmon country. I want to marry the sockeye Salmon." His sisters went with him in his canoe "Tupa'nk·ʟ." They travelled westward. When they reached the country of the Salmon, he told his sisters that he intended to carry away the chief's daughter, and he ordered them to make holes in the canoes of all the Salmon by pulling out the filling of the knot-holes. Then they went up to the house where he was invited, and feasted. After they had eaten, the Raven prepared to carry to his canoe the food that was left over. He said to the chief's daughter, "Will you please help me to carry my food to the canoe?" She did so, accompanying him down to the beach. He went aboard, and asked the girl to step into the water, in order to reach the canoe more easily. He induced her to step farther and farther, and finally took her into his canoe. Then his sisters struck the sides of the canoe "Tupa'nk·ʟ." with the palms of their hands, and it went of itself. The Salmon rushed to their canoes in order to pursue them; but after they had gone a short distance, their canoes foundered.

The Raven and his sisters carried away the young woman, and reached their home safely. The woman had beautiful long hair. Her husband asked her, "Where did you get that long hair?" She replied, "I pulled it and made it grow." Then the Raven said, "Oh, please pull my hair too, and make it grow!"—"No," she said, "I don't want to do it. If I should do so, your hair would become entangled in the salmon there drying over the fire, and you would pull them down." But the Raven insisted. Finally she grew angry, and said, "Well, I will pull your hair." She did so, and the Raven found that it reached down to his shoulders; but he was not satisfied, he wanted to have it longer. Then she pulled it until it reached down to his waist, but still he was not satisfied. He insisted, until finally she made it as long as her own hair. Then the Raven arose, intending to show himself to the people. While he was going out of the house, he moved his head from side to side, so that his hair flew about. When he passed under the drying salmon, they became entangled in his hair. He tried to pull it out, and finally succeeded. Then he went out and showed himself to the people. Soon he re-entered; and since he was still moving his head from side to side, his hair again became entangled in the salmon. He tried to disengage himself, but found it very difficult. Then he grew impatient, and said to the salmon, " I don't want to catch you a second time," and threw them out of the house. Then his wife arose and said, " I refused to make your hair long, but you insisted. I knew that you would maltreat the salmon." With this she jumped into the water, and all the salmon followed her. They swam back to the country of the salmon, and the Raven lost his long hair. Then he was very sad.

THE MINK.

Once upon a time there lived a woman named Nŭspusɛlxsak·ai'x· at Ts'ē'qoē, some distance up Bella Coola River. She refused the offer of marriage from the young men of the tribe, because she desired to marry Smai'yakila, the Sun. She left her village and went to seek the Sun. Finally she reached his house, and married Smai'yakila. After she had been there one day, she had a child, who was named T'ōtqoa'ya. He grew very quickly, and on the second day of his life he was able to walk and to talk. After a short time he said to his mother, " I should like to see your mother and your father;" and he began to cry, making his mother feel homesick. When Smai'yakila saw that his wife felt downcast, and that his son was longing to see his grandparents, he said, " You may return to the earth to see your parents. Descend along my eyelashes." His eyelashes were the rays of the Sun, which he extended down to Ts'ē'qoē. They descended along his eyelashes, and came to Ts'ē'qoē, where they lived with the woman's parents.

T'ōtqoa'ya was playing with the children of the village, who were teasing him, saying that he had no father. He began to cry, and went to his mother, whom he asked for bow and arrows. His mother gave him what he requested. He went outside and began to shoot his arrows towards the sky. The first arrow struck the sky and stuck in it; the second arrow hit the notch of the first one; and thus he continued until a chain was formed, extending from the sky down to the place where he was standing. Then he ascended the chain. He found the house of Smai'yakila, which he entered. He told his father that the boys had been teasing him, and he asked him to let him carry the sun. But his father said, " You cannot do it. I carry many torches. Early in the morning and late in the evening I burn small torches, but at noon I burn the large ones." T'ōtqoa'ya insisted on his request. Then his father gave him the torches, warning him at the same time to observe carefully the instructions that he was giving him in regard to their use. Early the next morning, T'ōtqoa'ya started on the course of the sun, carrying the torches. Soon he grew impatient, and lighted all the torches at once. Then it grew very hot. The trees began to burn, and many animals jumped into the water to save themselves, but the water began to boil. Then NûspusElxsak·ai'x· covered the people with her blanket, and thus saved them. The animals hid under stones. The ermine crept into a hole, which, however, was not quite large enough, so that the tip of its tail protruded from the entrance. It was scorched, and since that time the tip of the ermine's tail has been black. The mountain-goat hid in a cave, hence its skin is perfectly white. All the animals that did not hide were scorched, and therefore have black skins, but the skin on their lower side remained lighter. When Smai'yakila saw what was happening, he said to his son, "Why do you do so? Do you think it is good that there are no people on the earth!"[1]

Smai'yakila took him and cast him down from the heavens, saying, "You shall be the mink, and future generations of man shall hunt you."

Then Smai'yakila caused the waters to rise, so that they covered the whole country except a few mountains. The mountains SqtsL, SmaL, and Nusq!E'lst on Bella Coola River, and SimsEmta'nē near Bella Bella, were not covered by the waters. The Bella Coola and Bella Bella tied their canoes to the tops of these mountains, and for this reason they were not lost. The Ki'mxkuitx tied their canoe to the mountain Suwak·. The Taliō'mx· tied theirs to the mountain Asts'Elē'k·L. Some of the canoe ropes broke, and the people drifted away to distant countries. The deluge extended over the country of Skeena River; and the people of Nusmā'mt, the descendants of Tēqō'mnōL, drifted away from there, until finally they succeeded in tying their canoe to the mountain SqtsL.

Finally Smai'yakila caused the waters to subside, and the people descended from the mountains, and rebuilt their villages. The people of Nusmā'mt returned to Skeena River, and told their descendants that, since they had tied their canoe to the mountain SqtsL, the mountain belonged to them, so that they claimed two countries as their home, — the Bella Coola country and that of the Tsimshian. I think that one of the canoes drifted into the country of the whites.

After the water had subsided, Smai'yakila said, "I shall not make another deluge, and I will make the world beautiful." He told the porcupine that its meat should serve as food for man, and that the soup made of its meat should strengthen man, and prevent him from falling sick. And he said, "Your quills will be used for piercing the ears of women when they want to perforate them for the use of ear ornaments." And he gave the

---

[1] Iai'a tetō t'ai'x k·a k·'ás L'E'mstalalos?

marten its beautiful fur, and told the people to use it for blankets; and he taught them to make blankets of lynx and marmot skins; and he told the mountain-goat that man should use its hair for spinning and weaving, and that he should eat its meat; and he told the black bear that people should use its skin, and that man should eat its meat, while he forbade the women to eat bear meat; and he told the grisly bear that its skin should be used for blankets, and that its meat should be eaten by men and women.

Then the Raven instructed the people in the kū'siut ceremonials, while to others he taught the sisaū'k'.

THE DEER.[1]

The Deer said to his son T'ō'pewas, "Let us go in our canoe to fetch fuel." They launched their canoe, and paddled to the place where they were going to cut wood. The Deer went ashore, while his son remained in the canoe. He carried his stone hammer and his wedges to a large tree, which he began to fell. After he had left, two men and one woman passed by in their canoe. They stopped alongside of the Deer's canoe, and one of the men touched T'ō'pewas, feeling all over his body, and said to his companion, "He is good to eat."

The Deer, who was working in the woods, thought he heard a noise near his canoe; but the man stopped speaking, and it was quiet again. Therefore he thought he had been mistaken, and continued his work. After a while the strange canoe went on, and passed out of sight, behind a point of land. When the Deer had finished his work, he carried the wood to his canoe. He said to his son, "Did any people come here? I thought I heard some noise."—"Yes," replied T'ō'pewas, "there were two men and one woman; and one of the men touched me, felt all over my body, and said I was good to eat." Then the Deer grew angry. He said, turning his face toward the direction in which the canoe had disappeared, "Why do they say so?—those people who whistle through nose and anus, those long-tailed people." Then he returned to the woods to get more wood.

The woman in the strange canoe heard what the Deer said, and she remarked to her companions, "The father of that boy who you said is good to eat is scolding us." Her name was Nutsekoa'lsik·an, which means "long ear." She induced her companions to return. When they reached the canoe, they took hold of T'ō'pewas and killed him, biting him in the nape of the neck; then they devoured him.

Soon the Deer came back and found that his son had disappeared. Then he cried. The tears ran down his face. He threw the mucus from his nose down into the bottom of the canoe. Then he said to it, "Where is my

[1] See also Verhandlungen der Berliner Gesellschaft für Anthropologie, Ethnologie und Urgeschichte, 1895, pp. 193 ff.

13—MEM. AM. MUS. NAT. HIST., VOL. II. OCT., 1898.

son?" It did not reply, and he asked the thwarts. He asked the boards in the bottom of the canoe, and he asked the canoe line; but they did not reply. He asked the knot-hole. It answered his question, saying, "Those people whom you abused have returned, and have eaten him." Then the Deer was very sad. He paddled on, not caring where he went. He sang while he was paddling,—

> "Aʟnix'nĕ k'ōtsanĕ wasiai's tā mnatsai' anuswā'ʟax'dĕ, anuswā'ʟax'dĕ."
> ("It is calm, it is calm, but my child is dead.")

When he was rounding a point of land, he discovered many people. Then he stopped singing and rubbed his eyes, in order to brush away the tears. Now he saw a large village. Smoke was rising from one of the houses where a feast was going on. All the people had assembled in this house. They had built a large fire, on which they were heating stones. Two young men came out of the house and discovered the canoe of the Deer. They returned, in order to report to the host that a stranger was coming. The host told the people to wait before beginning to eat, because he desired to invite the stranger. When he came near, a person recognized him, and said, "Oh, I know him. He is a very good dancer. Invite him, by all means." The host sent a messenger to the beach to call him. The Deer went ashore and entered the house. On looking round, he discovered his son's blanket.

The host sent three messengers to the Deer, whom he told to sit down near the door. "We are informed that you are a good dancer, and we wish to see you dance." The Deer did not reply. He was sad because he had seen his son's blanket. After a short while he said, "How can I dance? All my paraphernalia are at home. If they were here, I should be glad to dance. I have no dancing-apron." The messengers asked, "What do you wear when you are dancing?"—"I wear knives made of mussel-shells tied to my arms." The messengers went and searched for shell knives, but they did not find any. Finally it occurred to them that an old woman who lived in the village was in possession of some shell knives. A messenger was sent to the old woman, who knew at once what they wanted. She gave them ten shell knives, five to be tied to each hand. The messengers sharpened them, and the Deer tied them to his hands. They gave him a dancing-apron. Then the Deer arose. He said, "Now I am ready to dance. Prepare your mats, and lie down. Soon you will be asleep. My dance will make you sleep. Take some boards and place them on your mats, because soon you will want to rest your faces on them." Then he stood up near the doorway, and, dancing around the fire, he sang,—

> "A'xkō tik'asᴇ'msmas aʟā'qula smā'o ti sxoā'xult wa sᴇ'msmas; aʟā'qula smā'o
>   ti sxoā'xult wa sᴇ'msmas aʟā'qula.
> Tsᴇntsitōmᴇ'lx'ax slā'ʟᴇmtsanai, sxoā'xults xoaxu'lt."
>
> ("I have no story. Only sleep is my story; only sleep, my story. Slumber, chil-
>   dren, sleep!")

Now they were all asleep. Then the Deer cut off their heads with his knives. Only one old woman had not been overcome with sleep. She ran about, calling the people, who awoke, and attacked the Deer. He jumped out of the house and ran along the beach, pursued by four men. When his pursuers gained upon him, he climbed a large tree. His pursuers sat down at the foot of the tree, and one of them said to his comrades, "Go home and ask the old woman if she does not know of some means of getting him down." One of the men went back, while the other three staid at the foot of the tree, watching the Deer. The messenger told the old woman that the Deer had climbed the tree, and asked her advice. Then she said, "Why don't you sing?"—"Teach me the song I have to sing;" and she sang, "Fall down, leg!"

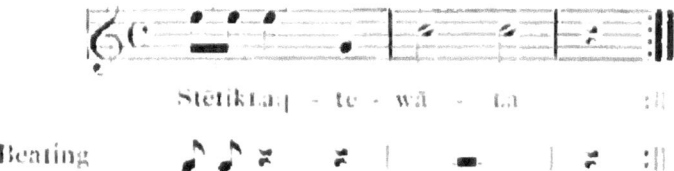

StétikÊla·] - te - wā - La   :||

Beating

The young man returned; but when he reached the tree on which the Deer was sitting, he had forgotten the song. Then they sent two men back to the old woman, hoping that the two would not forget the song. After they had learned the song, they returned. When they had nearly reached the tree, they jumped over a log; and as soon as they had done so, they had forgotten the song. Again they sent back two of the young men to learn the song. After the old woman had taught them the song, she advised them to continue to sing it while they were running back. They were humming the song all the time; and when they had nearly reached the tree, they jumped over a log. Immediately the song was forgotten. They returned again. Then the old woman said to them, "How does it happen that you always forget the song? Do you jump over a log?" When the old woman heard that they did so, she said, "You must go around the log." Now they returned, humming the tune all the way. When they reached the log that lay over their trail, they went around it. Now they remembered the song. They sat down at the foot of the tree and sang it four times. Then a leg of the Deer fell down. They sang again, and the other leg fell down. Now the Deer clung to the branches of the tree with his arms. They sang again, and an arm fell down. Now the Deer clung to the branches of the tree with his only remaining arm. They sang again, and the other arm fell down; and when they sang once more, the whole body fell down. They tore the Deer to pieces. One of the men took up one of the Deer's legs and said, "Later on some men shall have one leg shorter than the other one." That is the reason why some people limp.

THE HAU'HAU.

The Hau'hau lives on the mountain Nusla'xem, in a large cave. His cry is "Hauhauhau!" His wings are very large and beautiful. Some time ago the woods on the mountain were burned, and he moved away from it. He flew to Nulō'ʟk'ōʟ, on the north side of Bella Coola River, where is a stone pillar similar in appearance to a tree. There he put up his residence. Last year he was heard in Nulō'ʟk'ōʟ.

Once upon a time four men went mountain-goat hunting. In the evening they started a fire, and lay down to sleep, turning their backs toward the fire. One of them took his mountain-stick and placed it upright at his feet. Then they all went to sleep. Early in the morning the man who had placed his staff at his feet was awakened by the violent movements of his neighbor. He turned and looked at his friend, then he saw that he was dead. The two other men were also dead. He raised his head and looked toward the fire. Then he saw a long, slim hook coming out of the fire. He did not know what it was; but he soon discovered that it was a long beak. The beak came out farther and farther, and now he saw a neck as white as a swan's. Now it entered the arms of one of his friends. Then he knew that it was the Hau'hau who had killed his friends. He took his bow and arrow and hit the throat of the bird. After a little while the head came out again. Again he shot it. Thus he continued until all his arrows were spent. Then he took those of his friends. When almost all the arrows were used up, the sun arose; then the Hau'hau flew away, and the man thought he had not succeeded in killing him. Flying away, the bird shouted "Hä hä hauhaua niʟiʟakō'!" ("Our name is Hauhau!") The four men had camped on a small grassy slope over a precipice. The survivor crept to the precipice from where the beaks came. Then he saw many dead Hau'haus lying at the foot of the precipice. Some were very large, others were small. Then he knew that he had killed a great many, thinking that there had been only one of these beings. He returned to the village, and told the people that the Hau'haus had killed his friends, and that he had shot them. They buried the men, placing the bodies in boxes, which were put on the tops of poles which were surrounded by a fence.

THE WOMAN WHO MARRIED THE STUMP.

Once upon a time there was a woman who went into the woods intending to pick berries. She lost her way. Finally she reached a river. There she saw a wild-looking man approaching her. When he came near, she asked, "Who are you?" He replied, "My name is Stump." She asked, "Where is your house?" and he replied, "It is not far from here."—"Do you know where my father's village is?" she asked. He replied, "I know where it is.

but I shall not tell you. I want to marry you." The poor girl did not see any way of escape, and followed the Stump. Soon they reached a trail which led towards a patch of trees. Under these trees was the Stump's house. They entered and sat down.

After a short time Stump said to his wife, "Let us go outside. My head is full of lice, and I want you to louse me." She consented. The man went out first, and his wife was going to follow him; but when she was near the door, she heard some one calling her. She stopped, and on looking around she saw a woman who was rooted to the floor of the house. Her name was Nusqēēxtēɪ.pōtsā'ax. She gave her a brad-awl, and said, "Take this. The lice of which your husband is speaking are toads. Use this brad-awl to catch them. Don't be frightened and scream when you see the toads on his head. If you do so, he will certainly kill you. Catch the toads with this brad-awl, and throw them behind you. You must pretend to bite and eat the toads, but merely bite your nail, that your husband may be deceived by the noise." Then the woman went out and sat down at her husband's side. He put his head in her lap, and she began to look for lice. Then she saw the toads on his head. She took them up with the awl, threw them over her shoulder, and at the same time bit the nail of her thumb. Soon the man said, "What do I hear there? Are you biting the toads?" She replied in the affirmative. After a while the Stump requested her to stop, and they went into the house. Before they went to bed he said, "I am going away early in the morning." When the young woman awoke, she saw that her husband had left the house. Then she arose, went to the woman who was rooted to the floor, and asked, "Is there any hope of my escaping if I run away?" She replied, "You may try it, but your husband is keeping watch of you. His chamber-pot is his watchman, and it will tell him whatever happens during his absence."

Late in the evening the Stump returned. Then the woman pretended to be very happy to see him back home. In the evening he said again that he was going out early in the morning. The following morning the woman awoke again after her husband had left. Then she told the woman who was rooted to the floor that she intended to escape. As soon as she left the house, the chamber-pot called to its master, saying that his wife was making her escape. He heard it, although he was far away, pursued her, and took her back. On the following day the man went away again. Then the woman who was rooted to the floor told the young wife to take the fire-drill, and to make holes all round the rim of the chamber-pot. After she had done so, she gave her a bladder filled with urine, a comb, and a grindstone. Then she told her to run westward, and instructed her how to use the urine, the comb, and the grindstone. Now she left the house. As soon as she had left, the chamber-pot began to shout, but its voice was not so loud as before, because its rim had been drilled. Nevertheless the Stump heard the voice. He came home, and pursued his wife. When he approached her, she threw the bladder filled with urine over her shoulder and ran away. The urine was transformed into a lake, which detained the pursuer, who had to go around it. But soon he began to catch up with her again. Then she threw the comb over her shoulder, which was transformed into a thicket. The pursuer was unable to pass it, and had to go around it. But after a while he began to approach her again. Then she threw the grindstone over her shoulder, which was transformed into a large mountain, which carried her up to heaven.

When she reached heaven, she found a trail, which she followed. Soon she saw the house of the Sun, and on looking through a chink in the walls she saw a man (the Sun) sitting inside, who said, "Come in." The woman opened the door, but the doorway was blazing with fire, so that she did not dare to enter. The man told her to jump through the fire. She did so, and entered the house safely. After a short time the Stump reached the house. He looked in through a chink, and the Sun told him to enter. The Stump walked in, but he was consumed by the fire in the doorway.

The woman was invited to live in a room in one corner of the house. There she staid, and after some time she had a boy, the son of the Sun. He was called T'ōtqoa'ya. He was very ugly, and his face was covered with sores. After she had staid for some time, the owner of the house said to her, "Do you feel homesick?" and she replied that she longed to return to her father. Then the Sun bade her to look down, and he showed her the village from which she had come. She asked, "How can I return?" Then he told her to walk down along his eyelashes (the sunbeams). She took the boy on her back, and descended along the Sun's eyelashes. She reached her father's house in the evening. Her parents and friends were very glad to see her.

The next morning the boy went out of the house, and began to play with the other children, who made fun of him. Then he told them that his father was the Sun; but they merely laughed at him, until he grew very angry. Then he told his mother that he intended to return to his father in heaven. He made a great many arrows and a bow, went outside, and began to shoot his arrows upward. The first one struck the sky. The second one struck the notch of the first one. And thus he continued until a chain of arrows was formed which reached the ground. Then he climbed up; and, after reaching heaven, he went into the Sun's house. There he said, "Father, I wish to take your place to-morrow." The Sun consented, but said, "Take care that you do not burn the people. I use only one torch in the morning, and increase the number of torches until noon. In the afternoon I extinguish the torches one by one." On the following morning the boy took his father's torches and went along the path of the Sun; but very soon he lighted all the torches. It became very hot on the earth. The woods began to burn, and the rocks to crack, and many people died. But his mother waved her hands, and thus kept her own house cool. The people who had entered her house were safe.

When the Sun saw what the boy was doing, he caught him and threw him down to the earth, and said, "Henceforth you shall be the mink."

THE WOLVES.

There were two chiefs in the village Senxl. The name of the one was Senxalō'lɛla. The name of the other was Nutsxoä'sɛnɛm. They had two sons, who were gamblers. One day when they were playing, Senxalō'lɛla's son was winning all the time. Nutsxoä'sɛnɛm's son staked all his property and lost it. Finally he lost even his father's house. Then he staked his father, his mother, his wife, and he lost them. At last he had not even a blanket left. Then Senxalō'lɛla felt much annoyed. He told the people to leave the village, and to move to another place; and he ordered them to pack all their property, and to leave Nutsxoä'sɛnɛm's son to starve to death.

On the following morning the people took down the walls of the houses, loaded their canoes, and burnt what they were not able to carry away. They extinguished the fires, and deserted the young man. His sole property was the set of gambling-sticks by means of which he had lost his all. Before the people left, a friend of the young man had some glowing embers and hidden them in the sand; and before he went aboard he told his friend secretly where the fire was hidden. As soon as the people had started, the youth went, took out the glowing embers, and kindled a fire. He staid there for four days without partaking of any food. Then he began to feel the pangs of hunger. He went out and dug some clover-roots. Thus he kept himself from starving. He went about in the woods, gathering fuel for his fire, and moss to cover himself during the cold night.

One morning, when he awoke, he found that a heavy snow had fallen, and had extinguished his fire. Then he began to cry, and thought, "I wish I might die, because I cannot live without fire!" He lay down again under the moss, and cried until he fell asleep. The next morning he awoke, and he continued to cry. Finally he became so weak that he could hardly move.

One morning when he awoke, he heard the voice of a woman, who called him by name, and said, "What are you doing here?" He replied, "My father and his tribe left me to starve. I have been living here for nearly four months, and I am near death." Then the young woman stepped up to him and said, "My father sent me to invite you to his house." But the young gambler replied, "How can I accompany you? I am too weak even to turn over in my bed." The woman replied, "You may think so, but I know you are able to walk." Then the young woman took an object that looked like a strip of meat from her left breast, and gave it to the young man to eat. When he had eaten half of it, she asked, "Are you feeling better now? Try to turn over." The young man obeyed, and he found that the food had given him renewed strength. Then she made him eat the other half, and after he had done so she asked him to sit up. He tried to do so, and found that he was strong enough to rise. The young woman gave him another piece to eat, and after he had finished he was able to stand up, but he was not yet able to walk. The woman took still another piece from her left breast, and gave it to him. After he had finished eating, the young man had regained his whole strength. Then she patted his head with both her hands, and continued patting all over his body. Then his body, which had been very lean, appeared plump and fat. The woman said, "Now let us go to my father the Wolf. He is waiting for us. He told me to come and bring you home at once." They went on, and the young man felt stronger than he had ever been before.

Soon they reached the foot of a steep cliff. Here they stopped, and the young woman said, "This is my father's house. Take care! The door opens and closes its mouth. You have to jump in when it opens. I will go in first. Follow me when it opens its mouth again. When you enter, you will see me sitting at the rear end of the house. If I smile at you, you may come and sit down on my left-hand side; but if I do not smile, then stay in the doorway until you are asked to sit down. Beware of the door!" Now the door opened its mouth, and the young woman jumped into the house. When it opened its mouth again, the young man jumped in, and the door snapped behind him. Then he beheld the young woman sitting in the rear of the house and smiling at him. He walked up to her and sat down at her left side. He saw that the house was full of people, who were feasting. Above each man an object was dangling that looked like a wolf's tail.

After a little while the chief of the Wolves arose, and said to his people, "I have invited you, my tribe, to see my daughter and her husband; but they have been absent so long, that we finished the feast before they entered; but I am glad they arrived before you left my house. Now you may go." Then the men arose, took the tails that were dangling over them, put them on and went out in the shape of wolves. When leaving the house, they uttered a shrill howl.

The young man married the Wolf girl who had saved him. After some time they had a child. Then the young woman said to her husband, "You must be careful that the smoke never touches my blanket." The young man promised to do so.

One day one of the chief's sons said to his sister, "Let your husband go with us hunting mountain-goats." The woman asked him to accompany her brothers; but before he went she said, "I must give you strength before you start hunting." She patted his head and his body, and gave him a tail, saying that without the tail he would be unable to keep pace with her brothers. She also told him which way to go up the mountain, and instructed him not to follow her brothers. He obeyed her instructions, and soon found a trail of mountain-goats, which he followed until he came to a steep cliff. There he found forty goats. They were not able to proceed any farther on account of the precipice. He killed all of them. Then he rolled them down the precipice and returned home. When he reached the house, his wife smiled at him, and said, "How many goats did you kill?" He replied, "I killed forty;" but she did not believe him. She asked, "Where are my brothers?" He replied, "They went in another direction." While they were still talking, the two young men entered the house, and asked their brother-in-law how many goats he had killed. He told them of his success, and learned that they had not been able to kill any goats. Then the young woman asked her father to assist her in bringing home the meat of the goats that her husband had killed; and the whole Wolf tribe went, except the young man. He did not like being left behind, and thought, "I will go and see how they will bring the meat home." He followed them secretly; and when he came to the place where the dead mountain-goats lay, he saw that the Wolves were eating them. Then he ran home, and lay down, so as to make it appear that he had not left the house during the absence of the people. After a short time the old chief, his wife and her brothers, entered, each of them carrying something that looked like the windpipe of a large animal. They took off their load, and hung it on a pole over the fire. After a little while the woman took a mat from the corner of the house, and spread it on the floor at the left-hand side of the entrance. Then she took one of the windpipes down, opened one end, and began to pull out the meat of the mountain-goats. There was as much as the meat of ten mountain-goats in each windpipe. She emptied all of them, and the young man saw that they contained the meat of forty goats. They were the baskets of the Wolves. As soon as they were emptied, the windpipes disappeared. Then the Wolves dried the meat.

One day the two sons of the chief entered the house. One of them carried a ball about as large as a fist. He said, "We want our brother-in-law to play ball with us." The young man arose, intending to play with them; but the young woman said, "Take care! My brothers killed my first husband with this ball. They will let you catch the ball, and after you have caught it they will pursue you, and try to take it away from you. Then they will bite you from behind and kill you." But the young man did not listen to his wife's words, and followed his brothers-in-law. They began to play, and he was the first to catch the ball. Then he ran away, and his brothers-in-law pursued him. When one of them had almost reached him, and was just about to bite his neck, he threw the ball backwards, and thus saved his life. He went home and told his wife what had happened; and after that, when his brothers-in-law invited him to play with them, he refused.

One day his wife asked him to fetch water for her. He took the bucket and went down to the brook. There he met a pretty girl. They talked together, and he fell in love with her. Before they parted, he asked her to meet him at the brook every day. When he got home, his wife asked him for the water. She took it and said, "Now I will see if you have allowed the smoke to touch my blanket." She touched the left side of her neck with her finger, and the finger became red. Then she dipped the finger into the water, which was at once transformed into a thick jelly. Then she turned to her husband and said, "Did I not ask you not to allow the smoke to touch my blanket? But you did not obey my orders. You have fallen in love with a woman whom you met at the brook. If ever you do so again, I shall send you away. I pitied you before, but if you do not obey me, I shall send you back and let you starve." The man replied, "If you had told me plainly what you meant by not allowing the smoke to touch your blanket, I should have obeyed you. I should not have looked at any woman. I will promise you now not to look at or to speak to any woman hereafter." His wife continued, "Let us go to your father's house, that you may not see again the girl whom you met to-day." The young man was much pleased to hear this, because he longed for his own tribe. The next morning they made ready to start. The woman took one windpipe filled with food, and her boy carried it. After a short time they reached Nutsxoā'sɛnɛm's house. When they were approaching, they saw the old chief sitting in front of the house. He looked at his son, but did not recognize him. When they came nearer, the young man said, "Father, don't you recognize me?" When he heard his voice, the old man said, "Oh, my son! I am glad to see you, and I am glad to see your wife and your child!"

They settled in the house of the old man. After some time the woman asked her husband to fetch some water. He took the bucket and went down to the brook. When he was stooping down to fill his bucket, he heard somebody speaking. He turned round, and saw his former wife. It was the first time he had looked at her since his return. She railed at him, saying, "I think you are your wife's slave, that you do not even dare to speak to your own wife." But he replied, "At the time when my tribe left me, you would not stay with me, and you would not even give me a piece of dried salmon; but the wife whom I now have saved me, and therefore

I am her slave." The woman retorted, "Did you not gamble me away like a dog? And now I come back to you, and speak to you as a wife to her husband, for I love you dearly." Then he forgot the commands of his Wolf wife, and went to his former wife; but after a while she said, "Go back home now. I am afraid your wife may discover that we met." Then the man repented having disobeyed his Wolf wife's orders. He took the bucket home, but tried to hide it. She, however, said, "Give me the water. I want to see what you have been doing." She touched her neck with her fore-finger, and put her finger into the water, which was transformed into a jelly. She said, "What have you been doing? You have met your former wife." The gambler replied, "It is true. I met her at the brook, and did not want to speak to her, but she reminded me of our former love, and then I forgot my promise; but afterwards I regretted that I disobeyed you." His wife said, "I cannot forgive you again. Now I am going to leave you, and you may re-marry your former wife." The young man made up his mind to watch his wife, but the second night she and her son had suddenly disappeared. When the man discovered their absence, he arose and followed their tracks up the mountains. He followed them all day. In the evening he followed them by his scent. He was gradually being transformed into a Wolf, and a wolf's tail was growing on him. On the following morning he came to a bluff, and there he lost their tracks. He felt very sad, sat down, and began to cry. After a little while he heard an old woman addressing him, asking why he was crying. When he looked up, he saw an old Beaver, whom he asked, "Cannot you tell me if my wife and son have passed here?" The Beaver replied, "Do you see that cave? They went in there." He followed them, and reached a grassy slope, on which he found their tracks. He followed them again until he came to a beaver-dam. Here he lost their tracks again. Then he sat down and cried. Again he saw an old woman, who asked him why he was crying. When he looked up, he saw an old Beaver, who told him that they had entered the water. She said to him, "Go into the water, and don't be afraid if it reaches over your head. Keep on, and you will reach another world. There you will find your wife and son." He followed these instructions, and walked into the water; and when it closed over his head, he saw a light. He walked on, and soon reached dry land. There he discovered a small house. When he came nearer, he saw two old blind Wolves, a man and a woman, sitting in the house. He entered, and put some fuel on the fire. Then the old man said, "There is a stranger in this house." The gambler said, "Yes;" and the old man continued, "I know what brought you here. You wish to find your wife and son. Wait a while, and your boy will come here to play." He had hardly finished speaking, when the boy entered. As soon as he saw his father, he ran up to him. The father asked for his wife, and the boy replied that she was hidden in the latrine of his grandfather's house. Then the father said to him, "Go back to your house and begin to cry. When your grandfather takes you up, continue to cry, and ask for your mother. Continue until she comes out of her hiding-place." He followed his son secretly, and hid in one corner of the chief's house. Now the boy began to cry. The people came one by one, trying to quiet him, but nobody was able to do so. He continued to cry for his mother until she came forth from her hiding-place. Then the man jumped forward, saying, "I have followed you to your home, because I love you." Then the woman said, "Now I see that you really love me." And he continued to live with her in the country of the Wolves.

TRADITION FROM SNU'LLAL.

Once upon a time there was a chief of the SE'NOLLĒ whose name was Ga'watē. He had a son who was covered all over with scabs. The boy did not eat any thing but rotten salmon and fish-spawn, and drank the scum of old fish-bones which he boiled. When he had grown up, his father secured a wife for him from a chief of the same tribe; but when the young woman saw what kind of food her husband ate, she deserted him at once.

After a short time his father secured another wife for him, but she deserted him in the same way as the first one had done. He fared no better with the third wife, whom his father procured for him. After that, his father secured him a fourth wife, who staid with him two days; but she left him because he smelled just like rotten fish. Since all the pretty girls of the village refused to stay with him, his father thought, "I will give him a wife who is like him." The father found a girl whose body was also covered with scabs, and who lived on refuse. He secured her for his son, who married her. The young man and the woman loved each other; but the four young women who had deserted him teased them so, that the young man began to feel very badly.

One day he took a small box and filled it with tallow of the mountain-goat, and he took four sea-lion bladders filled with eagle-down. He put on a bear-skin blanket, took the box with the tallow and the down, and walked out of his house down to the river. When he reached the mouth of Bella Coola River, he went up the creek Tsäl. He was chewing a piece of tallow, and every now and then spat on the bushes which he was passing; and he blew eagle-down on to the bushes, which was held in place by the tallow. Thus he continued for four days. He did not hear any thing, and therefore he left the creek. Then he went up the creek Askal.t'a'. He did as before. He staid on the creek for four days; but since he did not see any thing, he left, and he went to the creek Sa'lemt. He did as before, but did not see any thing.   Then he resolved to stay in the mountains, and to die rather than to return without seeing a supernatural being.   He staid in the mountains for nearly a whole year.   Finally he came to a small spring, the water of which was very clear.   He noticed tracks, which showed that some animal visited the spring regularly.   He hid near by, and covered his head with his bear-skin blanket.   Soon he heard footsteps.   He looked cautiously out from under his blanket, and saw a man coming up to the spring.   He saw the man jump into the water and bathe, and then disappear again.   The youth resolved to stay at this place, and to observe the man who visited the spring. This man appeared every evening.   On the fourth day, when he arrived, he called the youth, saying, "Arise, and come here."   Then the youth arose. The stranger asked him, "Why did you come here?"   He replied, "I left my home because I am so ugly.   I had four wives, but they would not stay with me.   Then I took one who is just like myself, and she loves me ; but the other four have been teasing me all the time, until I went to the mountains, and now I want you to help me."   The man, who was no other than the Killer Whale, asked him what he had been eating, but the youth refused to reply.   Then the other ordered him to drink from the water of the well, and to take as much as he could.   The youth began to drink, and continued drinking until he was unable to swallow any more.   The stranger ordered him to sit down.   He patted his chest and moved his hands downward along his body, patting him all the time.   As soon as he began to pat his abdomen, the youth began to vomit rotten fish, salmon-spawn, and the scum of boiled fish-bones.   Then the Whale said, "That is the reason why your wives do not love you."   Now he rubbed the youth with the palm of his hand.   He ordered him to look in his face.   Then he pulled his hair and made it long, and he sprinkled it with the water of the well, which gave it a light brown color.   Finally he took four twigs of hemlock, dipped them into the water, and moved them up and down the youth's back four times.   Then his skin became white and smooth.   Then he moved them up and down the front of his body four times, and this also became white and smooth.   Then he said, "From now on your name shall be xwᴇ'laxusᴇm." He made the youth put on his bear-skin, which he covered with eagle-down, and he placed red cedar-bark round his neck.

The Glacier.

A mountain-goat hunter arose very early in the morning.   He put on his leggings and began to climb the mountains near Nukī'ts.   Very high up the mountain there is a river called Tsimī'lt.   Here he sat down, leaning on his arm.   He looked at the large glacier from which the river was coming.   Suddenly he saw a large fire coming forth from a cave in the glacier, and falling down near him. It rolled down the mountain. A thread of fire connected it with the cave. Suddenly it turned back, and disappeared in the cave from which it had come. The young man was very much surprised. He looked at the place whence the fire had come. After a little while it re-appeared, moving through the air over the sea, and then returned again into the glacier. Then the young man cautiously crept up to the point from which the fire emerged. Soon he saw it coming out again, and again it returned to the glacier. Then he thought, "I will take my stone knife and cut the thread which holds it to the glacier." As soon as it came out again, he cut the thread. The ball of fire fell down. He took it up and hid it under his blanket. Then he ran home as fast as he could. When he was near the village, he hid the fire in his quiver, which he tied up. The village in which he lived was very large, and behind the houses there was an open stretch of land. He hung the quiver on the branch of a tree when he entered his house. Early the next morning he arose, made a fire, and told his friends to call the people. He intended to show them what he had found. His friends went into all the houses and called the people. The young man told them to assemble on the open place behind the houses. He told them to arrange themselves in two rows opposite each other. Then he took his quiver and said to the people, "I shall open this. Do not be afraid. I shall throw to you what I have found, and you will throw it across to the people standing on the opposite side. Do not let it fall down, but let it fly to and fro." He opened the quiver. At once the fiery ball flew out, and they played ball with it, throwing it from one side to the other.

A very few people had staid in the houses, and when they heard the noise, they also came out to see what was going on. Only one old woman, who was unable to move, staid in her house. After a while the people grew tired of playing. They returned to their houses and took their meals, and then they returned to the open place and continued to play. They threw the ball to and fro, and whenever any one hit it, they shouted, "Wa!" The old woman was the only person who staid behind.

While the people were playing, a beautiful young man entered the village. He opened the doors of all the houses, but he did not see a soul. At last he found the old woman. He asked her, "Where are all the people?" She replied, "I suppose you have just arrived here, else you would know that a man found a wonderful ball of fire. All the people are playing with it behind the houses."—"Oh!" said the man, "that ball belongs to me. I am looking for it, and I came here to recover it." The stranger touched the feet, the legs, the body, and the head of the old woman. Then she lay there dead. He assumed her shape, took her staff, which was lying next to her, and left the house. Then he went to the opening where the people were playing. They saw him coming, and believed him to be the old woman. Then they laughed, and were glad to see her coming too. They told him to sit down, and promised to throw the ball of fire to him too. As soon as the ball was thrown to him, he took hold of it, spread his legs, and put it into his anus. He jumped up, tore off his skin, and appeared in his own shape as a beautiful young man. He was the glacier himself, and the fiery ball was his wind.

THE BLACK BEAR.

A chief's daughter went digging clover-roots. When she reached a place where many roots were growing, she began to dig. Then she stepped on some dung of a black bear. She sat down, and while cleaning her feet she scolded the bear. After a short time she saw a good-looking youth coming towards her. When he reached her, he said, "A short while ago you were scolding me. You said that my dung smelled very badly. Now let us see if yours is better than mine." He compelled her to defecate. The girl wore a neck ornament made of small coppers. She tore off a few of these, and dropped them unobserved. Then she said, "Behold, there is my excrement!" The bear did not believe her. He struck the small of her back, thus compelling her to defecate. Then he made her ashamed, saying, "Your excrement smells worse than that of any animal."

Then the youth, who was no other than the son of the chief of the Black Bears, took her to his own house and married her. One evening he sent her out to gather brushwood for their bed. She obeyed, and soon returned, carrying a heavy load of hemlock-branches. Then the man said, "We must not use this kind of bedding, else we shall have bad luck. Take it back." He went himself, and gathered devil-clubs. He loosened the soil for a space one fathom square, covered it with rotten wood, and spread the devil-clubs over it. Then he gave her to eat what she believed to be dry salmon, but it was skunk-cabbage. She ate it, and he said, "Now I see that you love me, for you eat my food without asking a question." Next he gave her dried goat-meat and bear-berries. After she had partaken of the food, he told her that what she had believed to be goat-meat was human flesh. After they had eaten they went to bed. It was in the fall of the year, and they slept until late in the spring. The chief's daughter thought she had been away a single night, but it had been a whole year. When they awoke, she saw devil-clubs growing all round their bed. Now they made a fire, and she sat at the right of the door, while her husband sat at the left. He asked, "Have you any relatives?"—"Yes," she replied, "I have parents, brothers, and a sister."—"And what are your brothers' occupations?" She answered, "The first is a canoe-builder; the second, a wood-carver ; the third, a singer, and master of ceremonies of the winter dance.   I am the fourth child, and I am a dancer.   My younger brother is a hunter.   The youngest of us is a girl, who is still playing."   Then her husband asked, "Is your brother the hunter old enough to fall in love ?" —" No," she replied, "he is too young."—"What kind of feathers does he use to wing his arrows ?"—"For small game he uses two grebe feathers, but for large game two loon feathers."   Then the Bear drooped his head and began to cry.   He said, "I know your brother is watching us now. He will kill me.   When I am dead, skin me, but be careful to leave my skin whole.   You shall wear it as a blanket."   He had hardly finished speaking, when an arrow struck him, and he fell dead.   Then two dogs jumped into the bear's den, followed by their master, who was greatly surprised to find his sister.   When he prepared to skin the bear, his sister stopped him, telling him of what had happened, and of the instructions the bear had given her.   She skinned the bear, and they started to go home. The woman insisted on carrying the bear-skin, although her brother thought that it would be too heavy for her.   While they were walking, the young man led the way.   His sister and his two dogs followed.   All of a sudden he heard his two dogs bark as though they had found a bear.   He turned back, but almost immediately the dogs stopped barking.   When he asked his sister about it, she replied that she had been playing with the dogs. The youth went on.   Soon he heard his dogs bark again, and he also heard the growls of a bear.   When he turned back, the noise stopped, and he saw nothing but his sister and his two dogs.   He begged her to hasten, but she asked him to proceed and not to mind her.   He went on.   After a short time the dogs barked again, and a bear was heard to growl.   Then the youth hid behind a tree ; and soon he saw a large bear coming, accompanied by two dogs.   Now he knew that his sister had assumed the form of a bear. Therefore he did not shoot her.   He ran back and intercepted his sister. who, as soon as she saw him coming, resumed her human shape.   Now they reached the village, and the young woman was heartily welcomed by her parents, her brothers, and her sister.

On the following day she prepared to clean and stretch the bear-skin ; but her brother objected, saying that it was customary to wait four days before doing this work.   She replied that she was following her dead husband's instructions, and that if she did not do so they would be visited by misfortune.   Her father asked his son to let her have her way.   The youth was afraid of her, because he knew that she had it in her power to assume the form of a bear; so he did not object any longer, but left the house during the night to go hunting in a distant valley.

The woman arose before the break of day, and, without stopping to take breakfast, she began to clean the bear-skin.   After this was finished, she awakened the people, asking for a bone needle with which to sew the skin to the stretching-frame. She was given one. After a short time she said, "My needle is broken. Give me another one." She sent her little sister, who was sitting near her, to get another one. She broke one needle after another. At last, when she sent her little sister to get another one, her mother sent word that she had no more needles. Then the woman began to growl like a bear. She put on the bear-skin, assumed the form of a bear, and killed her mother. Then she went through the whole village, and killed all the people except her little sister. After that she took off the bear-skin and hung it up. She sat down on the right-hand side of the fire, while her sister sat on the left-hand side. On looking at the bear-skin, the little girl observed that the woman had put all the broken needles into the jaws of the bear-skin to serve as teeth. Forte ante ignem pedibus passis sedebat cum subito menses facere coepit. Postea sorore arrepta vulvam capite eius detergebat simulque se eam ad id ipsum dicebat servasse. When the woman was sitting near the fire, she took out her lungs and put them into her left hand, and she took out her heart and put it into her right hand. She expected that her surviving brother would try to kill her, and she wished to deceive him. Since she had taken her heart and lungs from her chest, an arrow shot into her body would not kill her.

Then she went to sleep. While she was lying there, her brother returned. The little girl told him what had happened, and asked him to shoot through the hands of the bear woman. He did so, and she died. Then he ran away with his sister, fearing that the bear woman might revive. They crossed a deep canyon on a log. After they had crossed, he laid the log so that it must turn over when stepped upon. Soon the bear woman was seen following their tracks. She stepped on the log, which turned over, so that she dropped into the chasm below.

The youth and his sister travelled on. While they were walking, he said, "Let us try to find a village. There I will marry you." The girl agreed. Finally they reached a sheet of water. They saw a village on the other side. Then he shouted, asking to be taken across; and soon a canoe came in answer to his summons. When they had reached the village, the youth told the people that the bear woman was pursuing them, and that he had tried in vain to kill her. The people deliberated as to what to do, and finally decided that the Loon and Grebe should fetch her. The barnacles and sea-worms were to hide under the boards in the bottom of the canoe, and bite her, so that she would jump up and upset the canoe. Soon she arrived, and the people heard her shouting on the other side of the water. The Loon and the Grebe launched their canoe, which was very unsteady, and the barnacles and sea-worms hid under the boards in the bottom of the canoe. They went across, and the bear woman got aboard. When they were in the middle of the water, the barnacles and worms bit her. She jumped up, and the canoe capsized. The birds swam ashore. After a short time the barnacles and sea-worms came ashore too. They looked very stout, because they had eaten the bear. Then the youth said to the girl, "There are two trails here,—one leading to the left, the other to the right. You follow the one, I will follow the other. If the trails meet, we will marry; if they do not, we here separate forever. They started, and after a while met each other. Then the youth married the girl. (Mask of the Bear, Plate X, Fig. 12.)[1]

VI.

It is necessary to make a few remarks on the relation of the ceremonials of the Bella Coola Indians to their mythology. I have not seen any of their ceremonials, and my descriptions are based on inquiries, and upon the accounts published by Fillip and Adrian Jacobsen.

The Bella Coola have two ceremonials,—the sisau'k· and the kū'siut, which correspond to the Laō'laxa and the ts'ētsa'eqa of the Kwakiutl. I have described these ceremonials fully in another paper.[2] The sisau'k· ceremonials are mostly dramatic representations illustrating the clan legends, some of which have been recorded in Chap. IV, while the kū'siut ceremonials are dramatic representations of the initiation of members of various clans into certain secret societies. Among these, the Cannibal Society, the Society of the Laughers, and the Society of the Throwers, are the most important. These are called by the Bella Coola the ɛlaxō'lɛla, Olx, and Dā'tia. I described on pp. 34, 35, the spirits presiding over the two first-named societies. The information which I obtained on these points is perfectly clear and consistent. I cannot quite reconcile the explanations given by A. and F. Jacobsen to the accounts which I received. It seems that their accounts do not clearly distinguish between the opinions held by various tribes. In the article above referred to, I described fully the opinions held by the Kwakiutl in regard to the origin of their Cannibal Society. They believe that a spirit called Baxbakualanuxsi'waē initiates the Cannibals. He is represented as having an enormous black head with dilated nostrils and large mouth. I have made frequent inquiries among the Bella Coola, but received the uniform answer that this being does not initiate their Cannibals. It is not impossible that a few families may have adopted this tradition from the Kwakiutl tribes, but I have not been able to find it among the Bella Coola. Jacobsen maintains that Baxbakualanuxsi'waē is the particular spirit of the Cannibal among the Bella Coola, and brings forward the well-known

---

[1] Additional legends of the Bella Coola ...ve been published in the publications quoted on pp. 26, 27.

[2] Annual Report of the U. S. National Museum for 1895, pp. 311–738.

tradition of the Awī'k'enōx as an explanation of the ceremonial. The only modification which I note in this tradition is that the Cannibal's wife is described as sucking out through their ears the brains of children,—an incident which I heard related of the mother of Aʟk'unta'm.[2] He calls him "Beek-Beek-Kvalanit, and in the Bella Coola dialect, Päh-Päh Kualanusiva." This word is decidedly of Kwakiutl origin, meaning "the one who eats human flesh at the mouth of the river (or at the north end of the world)." Neither have I been able to find any mask representing this being among the Bella Coola tribe. The masks which they use in connection with the Cannibal ceremony are of quite a different character (Plate XII, Figs. 1–8). I am the more inclined to think that Mr. Jacobsen did not clearly distinguish between the customs and traditions of various tribes, since he introduces "Ganikilla Ko" (Qā'nig'ilak̆) in the traditions of the Bella Coola, while it is distinctively a legend of the Kwakiutl tribes of the extreme northwest of Vancouver Island. Jacobsen does not distinguish clearly between the sisau'k· and the kū'siut, stating that the kū'siut dances are performed during the sisau'k· in the same way as, among the Kwakiutl, a ʟaō'laxa may be celebrated during the ts'ē'ts'aēqa. This may be, but theoretically the two ceremonials must be considered entirely distinct. According to the information which I received, sisau'k· dances may be held in summer, in which case the kū'siut could not possibly form part of the sisau'k· ceremonial. When, on the other hand, the sisau'k· takes place during the kū'siut period, it would naturally be accompanied by kū'siut dances.

As stated before, the sisau'k· is a ceremonial in which the legend of the clan is illustrated by means of dramatic performances. At the same time valuable presents are distributed among the guests who are invited to witness the ceremonial. The value of the gifts amounts often to several thousand dollars. At this time the family legend is told in general outlines, but the details of the legend are kept a secret, and are transmitted only to those who are initiated in the sisau'k· of the clan. It seems that we must consider the transmission of the sisau'k· legend in the following manner: At any given time it is the property of the chief of the family, who, at the time of the celebration, transfers his rights to his successor, generally to his son. The full tradition is kept secret by the owner. It seems that there is a close analogy between the conditions prevailing in the northwest and those found among the southwestern Indians, among whom certain priests are guardians of traditions. Among the tribes of the northwest coast the chief of a family is the guardian and owner of the family tradition, while among the southwestern tribes the priest is the guardian of the tradition belonging to a clan or to a fraternity. My impression is, however, that among the northwestern

[1] Verhandlungen der Berliner Gesellschaft für Anthropologie, Ethnologie und Urgeschichte, 1891, p. 394.
[2] Ibid., 1894, p. 292.

Indians the tradition is considered much more clearly the property of the person who has it in charge than it is among the southwestern Indians. A description of the sisau'k· ceremonial has been given by Jacobsen in the paper above referred to.[1]

A clan legend which is illustrated in the sisau'k· ceremonial is called by the Bella Coola "Sᴇmsma" or "Smā'yusta." These traditions are the exclusive property of each clan. The laws according to which they descend from generation to generation differ from the laws prevailing among the other Coast tribes. The inhabitants of each Bella Coola village are not subdivided into clans, gentes, or septs; but each village community forms a unit, and possesses the same tradition. In order to keep the tradition in the tribe, the law requires that no person shall marry outside of his own village community. Thus the clan tradition is kept the exclusive property of the village community by means of endogamy. I have made very careful inquiries in regard to this point, and all the old men make substantially the same statement. Even marriages among near relatives are permitted; and although marriages of people who are distantly related, or not related at all, are preferred, it even happens that cousins marry, or that an uncle marries his niece, in order to keep the clan tradition from being acquired by another village community. It seems, however, that, owing to the influence of the Coast tribes, the endogamic system has begun to give way to an exogamic system. Powerful and wealthy chiefs marry outside of their own village community, in order to secure an additional clan legend through marriage. This new system agrees with the one prevalent among the Kwakiutl tribes.

The kū'siut, as stated before, is a religious ceremony in which all the deities of heaven are personified. The members of various clans are initiated according to their clan traditions; but the same societies and the same deities appear in the traditions of all the various clans. From what little I have been able to learn, it seems that there is an elaborate opening of the whole ceremonial, corresponding to the opening of the ceremonial among the Kwakiutl.[2] I received the following description of the opening ceremony:—

The person who invites to the kū'siut, that is to say, the man whose son is to be initiated into one of the secret societies according to the tradition of his clan, requests a person who is called Ē'xĕm to invite the nine brothers and their sister, who reside in the House of Myths, and in whose charge the kū'siut is placed. The names of the brothers are Xᴇnɪxĕmalā'oʟla, Xĕ'mtsiwa, Ōmq'ōmki'lik·a, Q'ō'mtsiwa, Aimalā'ōʟla, Ai'umki'lik·a, Kᵘlĕ'lias, Q'ulaxā'wa, Āt'māk{ᵘ}; and that of their sister, ʟ'ĕtsā'aplĕʟāna (see p. 33). In the rear of the house an elevated room is prepared for E'xĕm, in which he lies down. He is covered with rings made of red cedar-bark. For four days he stays

[1] Ymer, 1895, pp. 1-23.
[2] I have described this fully in the Annual Report of the U. S. National Museum for 1895, pp. 500 ff.

in this room. Then the host sends messengers to invite the people. They take staffs, and tie red cedar-bark round their heads, and go from house to house, singing, "Nūyaxdĕts wa nōnōsp'otstsē' he!" ("I wish to find some one who understands the winter ceremonial.") This they repeat in every house. Then they return to the host's house, who sends them out again, ordering them to sing, "Qōts'ak·ĭm totĕts wa nōnōsp'otstsē' he!" ("I wish the dancers would wash their hands.") Again they return to his house. They are sent out once more with the message, "Xoĕtsak·ĭmtotĕts wa nōnōsp'otstsē' he!" ("I wish the dancers would make their hands tremble.") They return once more to the chief's house, and are sent out again with the message, "Tapamak·tĕts wa nōnōsp'otstsē' he!" ("I want the dancers to look at their hands.") Now the dancers are ready, and come to the house. Then Ē'xĕm arises and dresses. He puts on a head-dress of birds' skins, ornamented with red cedar-bark. He is accompanied by women. Another man, who is called Nusx·ia'mʟ, adorns himself with red cedar-bark. He carries in his right hand a small baton covered with red cedar-bark. In his left he carries a larger stick, on which he beats time with the small baton. He sits down, and now all the people enter. First of all, Ē'xĕm comes in, accompanied by many women. Nusx·ia'mʟ begins to sing and to beat time, and Ē'xĕm shouts, "Ooo!" Ē'xĕm walks around the fire, keeping it to his left, and shaking his bark. Before he begins the circuit, he gives four jumps near the door. Four times he goes round the fire, and every time he reaches the door he gives four jumps. As soon as he does so, Nusx·ia'mʟ beats time slowly. When Ē'xĕm has finished his dance, the people take him to a place near the door, and a woman sings near him. Nusx·ia'mʟ and the people join her, then she dances her winter dance. Before she quite finishes, the people make her stop, and another woman begins her dance. Nusx·ia'mʟ beats time, and the other people join his song. The people make her stop again. Thus a great many people perform their dances. Now Ē'xĕm appears again, crying, "Ooo!" and Nusx·ia'mʟ beats time. Again he jumps four times to the right and four times to the left when reaching the door. After this, two more men and two more women perform their dances. After this has been done twice, Ē'xĕm stands near the door, looking upward, and says, "They are very near now." By this time the whole house is full of people. He goes around the house three times, dancing. Then he stays near the door, looking upward, saying all the time, "They are near by." When he reaches the door the fourth time, he cries, "They have arrived! Now they are here, dancing on the roof." Ē'xĕm continues to dance in the house, in order to induce them to come down. The first to come down is Xĕmxĕmalâ'oʟla, who stops at the rear of the house and sits down. Ē'xĕm continues to dance, and the others enter in order. Ē'xĕm stands near them and says, "Now I have placed them. Let the chief give them red cedar-bark." The people take small pieces of blankets, and sew red cedar-bark on to them in designs corresponding to the paintings on the faces of these deities, and they give these to the deities in order to appease them. Then they throw grease into the fire. During all this time Ē'xĕm stands in the rear of the house; and when a painting has been finished, the man who offers it to the deity shouts, "Xĕmxĕmalā'ōᴌᴌa t'aix·tau'!" ("This is Xĕmxĕmalā'ōᴌᴌa.") And Ē'xĕm sings, "Yayak·lamĕts'ĕk·a wa k'waᴌtᴇnai'x·aᴌ t'aix· tai'ya: aᴌt'aᴌ'ō'mataxstūs nusk·asiûtstaai'x· asᴇlkulatūtita'ya." As soon as he has finished his song, a loud noise is heard on the roof, as though a heavy stone were falling down. Ē'xĕm arises and performs a dance, while the noise of whistles is heard proceeding from him.

I am not familiar with the details of the ceremonial, and shall proceed to record the principal characteristics of the various societies. The Cannibal is initiated in the House of Myths by Bā'ᴇxōᴌᴌa. I recorded above (p. 34) how a young man was initiated by this spirit, and how he was returned to his friends. The return of the Cannibal is accompanied by ceremonies similar to those recorded in this tradition. It seems that the ceremonies of the Cannibals of various families are much alike, each having a tradition of its own referring to the initiation. It is believed that all the Cannibals, during their initiation, go up to the sky. I was told that on this journey they have to take human flesh along for food. It is said that in former times the chiefs held a council the night preceding the beginning of the ceremonies, and any one who wanted to show his liberality offered one of his slaves to be killed in order to serve as food for Bā'ᴇxōᴌᴌa. The offer was accepted, and a payment made for the slave. The latter was killed, and the members of the Bā'ᴇxōᴌᴌa order devoured one-half of the body before the departure of the novice to the woods.

The spirit appears to the novice while he is in the woods, and takes him up to the House of Myths, where he is initiated. Early one morning he returns, and is heard outside of the houses. He has lost all his hair except a little in the median line of the head. It is believed that it has been torn off by the strong wind blowing in the higher regions. Some Cannibals do not devour human flesh, but tear dogs to pieces or devour raw salmon. The ceremonial consists in pacifying the Cannibal, and exorcising the spirit that possesses him. This is the object of the kū'siut ceremonial. After a Cannibal has returned, the people try to capture him. When he is first heard to approach, the speaker, whose face is painted black, and who wears a cedar-bark ring, and is covered with eagle-down, shouts, "Tix·ma'ts'ᴇn tak·'axta'ᴌiᴌ, taaᴌ'ai'ōts'ai. P'alx·ĕxtsalatstᴇnai' tix·ma'ts'ᴇn tasiswalō'ᴌiᴌ t'aᴌ'aiōtst'ai'!" ("Arise, it may be our Cannibal. Awake!") The Cannibal is accompanied by four assistants, who are called Aᴌiᴌpa, and who from time to time utter the cry, "Hoip!" which is intended to pacify the Cannibal. They wear masks (Plate XII, Figs. 4 and 5). The people try to throw a noose over his head; but he throws it off, refusing to be captured. Then the people shout, "Ya'i!" beating time rapidly. The Cannibal tears the ropes that hold him, and disappears. Then the people follow him, and search for him until they find him. As soon as they approach, he attacks them, but gradually he becomes quieter. Then the speaker (Alk") invites the people to the dancing-house, saying, "Ip'a'nap kukusiau't!" That means, "Dance, dancers!" Now the Cannibal opens the door, accompanied by his assistants. He wears the mask shown in Plate XII, Fig. 3. At once a number of women arise, ready to surround him as soon as he enters the house. They are called Aɬaɬ'au'ɬtɛmx·. The speaker, who holds a staff, arises and shouts, "Ō ū yä'liwatimōtx Alqōɬayak·ai's!" That means, "Act like a real Cannibal." The Cannibal utters his cry, "Hoäaā, hoäaā, hoäaā!" ending with a long deep growl. He stays in the doorway for a long time. Then he steps into the house, turns his left shoulder outward once, bites one man on the right-hand side of the house, and one on the left-hand side, and then performs his circuit of the fire, leaving the fire to his left. In dancing he holds his fists in front of his chest, one on each side. He moves in a stooping position, raising his feet very high. He dances for four nights, during which time the people try to pacify him by means of songs and dances. After he has first been induced to enter the house, he becomes quieter. Then he tells the people what he has seen during his absence, and the song-leader makes a song on the subject. The women do not learn about the events that took place during his absence until they hear the song. After four days the ceremony of exorcising the S'a'ɬpsta (Plate XII, Figs. 6 and 7), the monster that possesses him, is performed. A large dish is ornamented with red cedar-bark; and the assistant of the S'a'ɬpsta (Plate XII, Fig. 8), by means of incantations, makes the Cannibal vomit the snake, or the wolf, or the eagle, that possesses him. Then he is seen to carry the head of the animal under his left arm, while the body is seen in the rear, being held by his assistants. Then this animal is seen to vomit flesh and blood into the dish which has been prepared for the purpose. The Cannibal's assistants cover the body of the animal with down, while they cry from time to time, "Hoip!" Then the people beat time very rapidly, and suddenly the S'a'ɬpsta has disappeared. The people beat time four times, and after this the Cannibal has become like an ordinary man. He walks around the fire, which he keeps to his right, and says, "Now Bī'ɛxōɬla has left me." The contents of the dish are thrown into the water, but the dish itself is burned in the dancing-house. It is supposed that it is thus conveyed to heaven. After the dish has been burned, the Cannibal does not dance any more. Then a bed is prepared for him in the rear of the house, in which he must stay for four days. After this, he is allowed to re-enter the houses; but before doing so for the first time, he must stop at the door and shout, "Wa, wa, wa!" Then he jumps over the threshold. Accompanied by many men, he is led, after four days more, to the river for final purification. He is pushed into the water, but struggles to free himself. He tries to duck his companions, and utters his cries. Finally he is led back. Then he weeps, because the spirit has left him entirely. The people beat time while he is going back to the house. Then he is offered a piece of salmon, which is placed on his throat, while the people shout, "Hoip, hoip!" The salmon is taken away again, and after some time he is allowed to take one bite. Then he must lie down. After the dancing season is ended, he is again allowed to eat in the same way as other people do. The piece of salmon that was placed on his throat is eaten by children as a protection against sickness. Finally a ceremony is performed which is called "taking the lip of the S'a'ʟpsta out of the Cannibal's body." While this is being done, the people cry, "Hoip!" Then they throw the lip upon another Cannibal, who at once falls into an ecstasy. Then the shaman takes it back and throws it up towards the sky, where it disappears. The dish and the spoon that the Cannibal used during his ecstasy are destroyed. For four years he must wear a small ring of red cedar-bark, in summer as well as in winter.

The Ōlx is also initiated in heaven by the being described before (p. 35). There are different traditions regarding his initiation among different clans. Some Ōlx, during their performances, walk ropes which are stretched through the house. When he returns from his initiation, small whistles, called čaʟi'laxa, which imitate the voices of eagles, are heard outside of the houses. Then the Ōlx enters in a state of ecstasy, scratching the people who assemble to hold him, and tearing their blankets. Finally the people succeed in placing a blanket over his head, and he begins to come to his senses. When he enters the house, the people beat time, then he teaches the chorus-leader a song. The mask worn by the Ōlx is quite large, and characterized by a large nose (Plate XII, Fig. 9). He carries a dancing-club (Plate XII, Fig. 10), and rings made of red cedar-bark. He is accompanied by two assistants, who also wear masks.

VII.

We will now discuss the probable origin of the mythology described in the preceding pages. In order to do so, it is necessary to make a brief statement in regard to the social organization of the neighboring tribes. In another paper[1] I have fully discussed the considerable amount of borrowing that has taken place among the Coast tribes, and the relation of their

---

[1] Indianische Sagen von der nord-pacifischen Küste Amerikas, Berlin, 1895, pp. vi + 363.

mythologies to those of the interior. It is unnecessary to revert to this subject here. The similarity of the Bella Coola legends to those of the other Coast tribes on the one hand, and to the traditions of the Athapascan tribes on the other, is evident.

It is, however, important to compare their social organization with that of the neighboring tribes, in order to gain a clearer understanding of the origin of their peculiar organization. As stated before, the Bella Coola are divided into village communities, which are organized on an endogamic basis. Each village community has its tradition, which is represented in certain ceremonies. The supernatural beings which play a part in these traditions are personified by certain dancers. Other Coast tribes have a much more complex organization. The Tlingit and Haida are divided into two clans, each of which is subdivided into a great many families, which, as it would seem, were originally village communities. This opinion is based on the fact that the names of many of the families must be translated as "inhabitants of such and such a place." The two clans are present in all the villages of the tribe, each family belonging to either one clan or the other. The Tsimshian have the same system, except that the number of clans is four instead of two. Each tribe is divided into families, which embrace the inhabitants of a certain region ; but all the families of the whole tribe are classified according to the four clans. Among the Haida, Tlingit, and Tsimshian, descent is purely maternal ; among the northern Kwakiutl tribes, conditions are somewhat different, according to observations made by Dr. Livingston Farrand. Here we have village communities which are subdivided according to four clans in the same way as those of the Tsimshian, but descent is not purely maternal. There is a strong preponderance of the latter form of descent, but parents are at liberty to place their children in either the paternal or maternal clan. The preponderance of maternal descent is, however, so strong, that from my previous occasional inquiries I drew the inference that descent was purely maternal.

Among the southern Kwakiutl tribes the families constituting a village community are subdivided into a number of clans, but each clan is confined to one village. We do not find a limited number of clans pervading the whole tribe, as we do among the northern tribes. An analysis of the social organization of this tribe has shown that the present organization has evidently developed from a previous simpler state, in which the tribe was divided into single village communities. The present more complex organization resulted from the amalgamation of various villages. Owing to the influence of the totemism of the northern tribes, each village community adopted a crest, which in course of time became the totem of the clan.[1] The Kwakiutl have a peculiar organization, which may be considered a transitional stage between

---

[1] "Secret Societies of the Kwakiutl Indians" (Report of the U. S. National Museum for 1895, p. 332).

maternal and paternal institutions.   Descent is in the paternal line ; but a man, at the time of his marriage, receives his father-in-law's crest as a dowry, which he holds in trust for his son, so that actually each individual inherits the crest of his maternal grandfather.   The clans are exogamic.

The organization of the Salish tribes of the southern coast, who are linguistically closely related to the Bella Coola, is somewhat similar to that of the Kwakiutl.   They are divided into village communities, a few of which have amalgamated, as, for instance, among the Salish tribes of Vancouver Island, among whom the tribe consists of a number of septs, each of which owns a separate village.   Here the influence of northern totemism is very much weaker.   While most of the village communities have certain crests, these do not play so important a part in the social life of the tribe or in its mythology as they do among the Kwakiutl, and the village communities are not exogamic.   The Salish tribes of the interior are organized in very loose village communities without any trace of totem.

The fundamental difference between the northern tribes and the southern tribes consists, therefore, in the fact that the northern tribes have a limited number of clans which are present in all the villages, while among the southern tribes the village community is the only unit of organization.

The organization of the Bella Coola resembles most closely that of the Coast Salish tribes of southern British Columbia.   In both cases the tribe is divided into village communities, which possess crests and traditions.   This latter feature is, however, very much more strongly developed among the Bella Coola than among the southern tribes.   They differ in their laws of intermarriage.   While among the southern Coast Salish tribes there is a tendency to exogamy, the Bella Coola have developed a system of endogamy.

The tribes of the Coast Salish of the Gulf of Georgia claim descent from mythical ancestors, who are believed to have originated at the place which the tribe now inhabit.   A number of traditions of this kind bear evidence of having been derived from historical events.   Some of the tribes in the delta of Fraser River, have traditions which refer to the amalgamation of tribes who descended from the mountains, and who are described as the descendants of animals living in the mountains, and of the natives of the delta.[1]   I believe that the tribal traditions of the Bella Coola which were told in a previous chapter also bear evidence of the historical fates of the tribe.   It is very remarkable that the important tradition of Tôtosŏ'nx gives Fraser River as the place to which he descended from heaven.   In another tradition, Bute Inlet is given as the place at which one of the Bella Coola tribes originated. In still another one, Skeena River is mentioned as the home of one of the tribes (see p. 69).   I do not doubt that these allusions to territory

---

[1] Ninth Report of the Committee of the British Association for the Advancement of Science on the Northwestern Tribes of Canada, 1894, p. 3.

inhabited by Salish tribes refer to the early separation of the Bella Coola tribe from the related tribes of the Gulf of Georgia, and that in their traditions they have retained the memory of the emigration of part of the tribe from the southern territory. It seems also probable that the allusion to the origin of one family of the tribe on Skeena River refers to a mixture with the tribes inhabiting northern British Columbia.

The traditions of the tribes also describe the style of house used by the ancestors of certain village communities; and it is interesting to note that some of these houses correspond to the subterranean lodges that were in use among the Chilcotin, while others correspond to the tents that were in use among the Carriers. It is said that the ancestor of the Nullē'ix used the subterranean lodge which is called tsı'pa (see p. 87), while the ancestor of the Nusq!ɛ'lst used the skin lodge which is called sk·ma (see p. 64).

Since the Bella Coola retain the fundamental traits of the social organization of their congeners in the south, and since their traditions bear evidence of an emigration from that region, and since, furthermore, the linguistic evidence proves that the Bella Coola and the Coast Salish at one time inhabited contiguous areas on the coast, we are justified in assuming that the general culture of the Bella Coola at the time of their emigration must have resembled that of the Coast Salish. The question then arises, How did the peculiar endogamic system and the remarkable mythology of the Bella Coola originate from the much simpler forms that we find among the Coast Salish?

One of the most remarkable features in the inner life of the tribes of the northern coast of British Columbia is the great importance of the clan legend, which is considered one of the most valuable properties of each clan or family. It is carefully guarded in the same way as material property, and an attempt on the part of a person not a member of the clan to tell the tradition as his own is considered one of the gravest offences against property rights. The possession of a clan tradition is felt by the Indian to be one of his most important prerogatives. When, therefore, the Bella Coola settled on Bella Coola River, and were thrown into contact with the northern Coast tribes, the lack of a well-developed clan tradition must have been felt as a serious drawback. The physical appearance of the Bella Coola proves that at one time they must have intermarried to a great extent with the Bella Bella. Through these marriages the peculiar customs of the Coast tribes were first introduced among them. This is shown by the fact that a great many of the mythological names can be proved to be of Kwakiutl origin, of which stock the Bella Bella are a branch. Thus the name for their supreme deity, Smai'yakila, is a Kwakiutl word meaning "the one who must be worshipped." The name Ō'mq·ōmkilik·a is also of Kwakiutl origin, and may be translated as "the wealthiest one." The great frequency of words of Kwakiutl derivation will become clear by a glance at the following list, which contains words that can be proved to be of Kwakiutl origin :—

a'ᴌokoala = shaman.
Alk" = speaker.
E'mask'in (p. 49) (Kwakiutl, Hē'mask'in) = the greatest chief.
Hau'hau (p. 100) = a fabulous bird.
ᴌ'ā'qoag'ila = the copper maker.
ᴌ'ā'qumēiks = sister of Masmasalā'nix (the ending, iks, designates "woman" in Kwakiutl).
ᴌēqumaii' = mythological name of deer.
Mā'ᴌak'ilaᴌ.
Mɛntsi't (p. 48).
Mīa'ᴌtoa = the country of the salmon (p. 38) (Kwakiutl, mē) = salmon.
Nō'akila (pp. 49, 66).
O''mɛaᴌk'as (p. 70) = the real O''meaᴌ.
O''meaᴌmai (p. 70).

Oaq'ōmki'lik'a (p. 33) (Kwakiutl, Q'ō'mq'ōmkilik a) = the wealthiest one.
Pō'ᴌas.
Qanāatsla'qs (p. 49).
Q'ōmō'qoa (p. 52) = the wealthy one.
Q'ō'mqūtis (p. 49) = rich at opposite side of river.
Q'ō'mᴌsiwa (p. 33) = wealthy at mouth of river.
Smai'yakila (p. 29) = the one who must be worshipped.
si'sinᴌ = a fabulous fish or snake (pp. 28, 44, 48).
Smayalō'oᴌla (p. 29).
T'ō'pewas (p. 97) = the fawn.
Winwī'na (p. 38) = war.
Wa'k'iᴌɛmai (p. 50) = the greatest river.

With these names and customs the clan traditions must have found their way to the Bella Coola, but their social organization differed fundamentally from that of the Bella Bella branch of the Kwakiutl. While the latter, owing to intimate contact with the northern tribes, had adopted the four-clan system with prevalent maternal descent, the Bella Coola were still distinctly divided into village communities that were not exogamic. It seems very likely that the jealousy with which the ownership of a clan tradition was guarded by the Coast tribes was very early introduced among the Bella Coola. Two means were available for preventing outsiders from acquiring the traditions. Among the Coast tribes with prevailing maternal institutions, among whom a limited number of clans existed, the ordinary law of inheritance was sufficient to retain the tradition inside of the clan. Not so among the Bella Coola. If their organization at an early time was similar to that of the Coast Salish, it is likely that the child was counted as well a member of the father's as of the mother's family, although the young woman generally moved to the village occupied by her husband. If the child belonged to the families of both parents, it had the right to use the tradition of either family ; and consequently in the course of a few generations, the traditions acquired by each family would have spread practically over the whole tribe. There were only two methods possible to avoid this result. The one was to prevent marriages outside the village community ; and this method would seem to have been most natural for a tribe organized in village communities, members of which were allowed to intermarry. The other method would have been to regulate the laws of inheritance in such a way that the child had to follow either father or mother, but that it had not the right to use the property of both parents. It seems to my mind that the former method was more likely to develop under the existing social conditions, and that to this reason we must ascribe the development of an endogamic system among the Bella Coola. The occurrence of endogamic marriage among this tribe is quite isolated on the Pacific coast. All the other tribes have exogamic institutions, and by this means preserve their property rights. It is interesting to note that the southern Kwakiutl, who originally seem to have been organized in village communities, have adopted exogamic institutions; but there is a notable difference, in the organization of the village community, between the Bella Coola and the Kwakiutl. Among the Bella Coola we generally find four ancestors to each village,—usually three men and one woman. It is true that these are generally called brothers and sister, but they were created independently by Sɛnx, and are therefore not necessarily considered as blood relations. Among the Kwakiutl the village community are considered the descendants of one single being; consequently, among the latter tribe they are all relatives, who are forbidden to intermarry; while among the Bella Coola they are not relatives, and may intermarry.

My inference is, therefore, that the curious social system of the Bella Coola developed through the influence of the customs of the Coast tribes upon the loose social unit of the Salish village community. The possession of clan traditions was felt as a great advantage, and consequently the desire developed to possess clan traditions. These were acquired partly by inter-marriage with the Coast tribes, as is shown by the fact that many of these traditions are borrowed from these tribes, partly by independent invention. The desire to guard the traditions which were once acquired led to the development of endogamic institutions, in order to prevent the spread of the traditions over the whole tribe.

The jealousy with which the traditions are guarded has had the effect of making each family try to prevent other families from knowing its own clan tradition. For this reason the clan traditions of the whole tribe are remarkably inconsistent. We find, for instance, that the well-known raven legend of the northern Coast tribes has been utilized by many families as a family tradition. But while one family uses one part of the tradition, other families use other parts of the same tradition. Thus it happens that among the Bella Coola we find the most contradictory myths in regard to important events in the world's history. Some families maintain that the Raven liberated the sun, while, according to another one, the Mink was essential in bringing about the present state of affairs. Still others say that Tōtosō'nx, during his travels, caused the sun to appear. The discrepancies in the traditions referring to the visit of the Mink and Wasp to their father, the Sun, are also very remarkable. Although a considerable amount of contradiction is inherent in all the mythologies of the North Pacific coast, they nowhere reach such a degree as among the Bella Coola; and I presume the fact that the traditions are kept secret by the various families accounts for this curious condition.

The prayers of the Bella Coola directed to Senx or Ta'ata bear a remarkable resemblance to the prayers of the Tsimshian addressed to Laxha, the sky. In both tribes we find the idea that when the Sun wipes his face it will be clear weather, and man will be happy; consequently the prayer to the deity "to wipe his face" occurs quite often.

One of the most important customs that the Bella Coola borrowed from the Coast tribes is the kū'siut ceremonial, with which are connected the various secret societies, particularly the custom of ceremonial cannibalism. The ceremonies and the paraphernalia used by the Bella Coola and by the Kwakiutl are practically identical. I told above (p. 34) the legend explaining the origin of cannibalism. Among the Bella Bella and Kwakiutl, another tradition is told to explain the origin of this custom. The tradition tells of a spirit called Baxbakualanuxsī'waē, who lives in the forest, and who initiates the members of the Cannibal Society. The series of traditions clustering around this being differ fundamentally from those referring to the Cannibal Society of the Bella Coola. The custom has also spread to the Tsimshian, who say that the secret societies were introduced by a hunter who was taken into the inside of a cliff by a white bear. Inside he saw a house, in which the various societies were performing their ceremonies. It appears, therefore, that the same ritual which is practised by three distinct tribes is explained by three fundamentally distinct myths; and we must conclude that in this case the ritual is older than the myth,—that the latter has been invented in order to explain customs that were borrowed from foreign tribes, so that the ritual is the primary phenomenon, while the myth is secondary.[1]

These considerations explain some of the psychological motives for the development of certain traditions and myths, as well as the curious inconsistency of the clan traditions of the Bella Coola. They do not, however, explain the most fundamental characteristic of the traditions of the tribe. I pointed out in the third chapter of this paper, that, notwithstanding the numerous contradictions contained in family legends, the conception of the word and the functions of the various deities are so well defined that we must consider the mythology of this tribe vastly superior to that of the neighboring tribes. While the latter believe in a great many spirits which are not co-ordinated, we have here a system of deities. The existence of a systematic mythology among the Bella Coola proves that under favorable conditions the advance from the lower forms of beliefs to higher forms may be a very rapid one.

---

[1] See Report of the U. S. National Museum for 1895, pp. 660 ff.

Our analysis shows that this system cannot be considered as an importation, but that it probably developed among the Bella Coola themselves. After they removed to their new home, a mass of foreign ideas had come into their possession through contact with their new neighbors. While these new ideas were being remodelled and assimilated, they stimulated the minds of the people, or of a few members of the tribe, who were thus led to the formation of an elaborate concept of the world. The concept which they have developed agrees in all its main features with those created by men of other zones and of other races. The mind of the Bella Coola philosopher, operating with the class of knowledge common to the earlier strata of culture, has reached conclusions similar to those that have been formed by man the world over, when operating with the same class of knowledge. On the other hand, the Bella Coola has also adopted ready-made the thoughts of his neighbors, and has adapted them to his environment. These two results of our inquiry emphasize the close relation between the comparative and the historic methods of ethnology, which are so often held to be antagonistic. Each is a check upon rash conclusions that might be attained by the application of one alone. It is just as uncritical to see, in an analogy of a single trait of culture that occurs in two distinct regions, undoubted proof of early historical connection as to reject the possibility of such connection, because sometimes the same ideas develop independently in the human mind. Ethnology is rapidly outgrowing the tendency to accept imperfect evidence as proof of historical connection; but the comparative ethnologist is hardly beginning to see that he has no right to scoff at the historical method. Our inquiry shows that safe conclusions can be derived only by a careful analysis of the whole culture. The growth of the myths of the Bella Coola can be understood only when we consider the culture of the tribe as a whole. And so it is with other phenomena. All traits of culture can be fully understood only in connection with the whole culture of a tribe. When we confine ourselves to comparing isolated traits of culture, we open the door to misinterpretations without number.

If, then, the demand is made for a more critical method in the comparative study of ethnology than it has generally been accorded, it does not imply a deprecation of the results of the method. When the human mind evolves an idea, or when it borrows the same idea, we may assume that it has been evolved or accepted because it conforms with the organization of the human mind; else it would not be evolved or accepted. The wider the distribution of an idea, original or borrowed, the closer must be its conformity with the laws governing the activities of the human mind. Historical analysis will furnish the data referring to the growth of ideas among different people; and comparisons of the processes of their growth will give us knowledge of the laws which govern the evolution and selection of ideas.

Reprint Publishing

For People Who Go For Originals.

This book is a facsimile reprint of the original edition. The term refers to the facsimile with an original in size and design exactly matching simulation as photographic or scanned reproduction.

Facsimile editions offer us the chance to join in the library of historical, cultural and scientific history of mankind, and to rediscover.

The books of the facsimile edition may have marks, notations and other marginalia and pages with errors contained in the original volume. These traces of the past refers to the historical journey that has covered the book.

ISBN 978-3-95940-200-2

www.reprintpublishing.com